During the twenty-nine years of an inspiration to his contempo countless ministers. Often, sitting in St Peter's Church in Dundee, I have wanted to ask the walls to tell me stories of the remarkable ministry he exercised within them between 1836 and 1843. Walls cannot speak, but books can. And while there are several excellent works on M'Cheyne, Jordan Stone has found a fresh way of bringing his story to life again. Here we are given glimpses of his personality, his devotion to Christ, the character of his ministry, the theology that gripped him, and the friends who surrounded him. Whether you have read everything you can about Robert M'Cheyne or have never heard his name before you will find both pleasure and challenge in Dr Stone's wonderfully readable *A Holy Minister*.

SINCLAIR B. FERGUSON
Chancellor's Professor of Systematic Theology, Reformed Theological
Seminary, Jackson, Mississippi

*A Holy Minister*, Jordan Stone's latest account of the animating commitments of M'Cheyne's life and labors, does more than repeat the well-rehearsed contours of his biography. Instead, it locates M'Cheyne amidst the galaxy of stars that shone in the Scottish church in the first part of the 19th century, and opens to our view the theological convictions and spiritual impulses that made his light burn with particular brightness. The piety of M'Cheyne, pulsing with love to Christ, is his great legacy, and Stone helps us to understand it in M'Cheyne and to long for it in ourselves. It is not to make much of M'Cheyne that we should read this book, but to learn from M'Cheyne how a revived ministry will ordinarily be the instrument of a revived church.

DAVID STRAIN
Senior Minister, First Presbyterian Church, Jackson, Mississippi

Robert Murry M'Cheyne's impact upon the Church cannot be over-estimated. From his annual Bible reading plans to his model of godliness, many have been encouraged by a brother who has long since joined the Church Triumphant. Jordan Stone's insightful and inspiring look at the life of Robert Murray M'Cheyne, especially his motivations for godliness and service, will serve anyone and everyone who reads this volume. But know that there is danger in picking up this book. You will not only be inspired, you will be challenged. This book is worth your time because Stone seems to 'know' M'Cheyne with understanding, and M'Cheyne 'knew' Jesus with understanding. Christ's beauty and preciousness shined throughout M'Cheyne's life and ministry, as evidenced on every page of this book.

JASON HELOPOULOS
Senior Pastor, University Reformed Church, East Lansing, Michigan
Author of *A Neglected Grace: Family Worship in the Christian Home* and *A New Pastor's Handbook*

With an economy of words and an extensive acquaintance with M'Cheyne, Jordan Stone explains the doctrines, biblical texts, people, and controversies that influenced him. This alone makes *A Holy Minister* a valuable book. But far more valuable is the care taken to show how M'Cheyne's personal piety, preaching, and pastoral ministry flowed from his deep love for the Lord Jesus Christ – the very love I want every seminarian to cultivate and cherish.

CHARLES M. WINGARD
Associate Professor of Practical Theology and Dean of Students,
Reformed Theological Seminary, Jackson, Mississippi

In terms of accessibility and usefulness to contemporary ministry I can think of no better book on M'Cheyne. Comprehensive and yet easily read, it does not shy away from tough issues like how to deal with controversy. In an age when charisma and giftedness put character and holiness to the side *A Holy Minister of Christ* is a needed corrective. A must-read also at a time of high-profile Christian leadership scandals, we have in M'Cheyne a model of humble holiness.

DAVID MEREDITH
Mission Director, Free Church of Scotland

Pastors need living mentors. They are essential to training and sustaining a pastor in his ministry. But it is also crucial that pastors have mentors from ages past who possess a wisdom and example from a different era. Robert Murray M'Cheyne is one of those unique voices. This is why

Jordan Stone has done every pastor a great service with this book, *A Holy Minister: The Life and Legacy of Robert Murray M'Cheyne.*

Stone brings to life a pastoral voice few outside of Scotland have heard, but every pastor needs. This book is a very concise, well-written, and accessible work that will act as a great introduction to Robert Murray M'Cheyne or a sweet reminder to those who already know him. I commend M'Cheyne to every pastor and this excellent work to get you started.

BRIAN CROFT
Executive Director, Practical Shepherding, Senior Fellow,
SBTS Church Revitalization Center
Author of *Facing Snarls and Scowls: Preaching through Hostility, Apathy, and Adversity in Church Revitalization*

*A Holy Minister* features the vibrant spirituality and pastoral fervor of Robert Murray M'Cheyne. Stone has carefully studied and now winsomely presents this great example to ministers today. Let us pray for a generation of pastors who treasure Christ the way we see modeled in this work.

Matthew Boswell
Pastor, The Trails Church; Hymnwriter; Assistant Professor of Church Music and Worship, The Southern Baptist Theological Seminary

# A Holy Minister

## The Life and
## Spiritual Legacy of

# Robert Murray M'Cheyne

# Jordan Stone

**MENTOR**
Encouraging Christians to Think

Copyright © Jordan Stone 2021

paperback ISBN 978-1-5271-0646-8
epub ISBN 978-1-5271-0739-7
mobi ISBN 978-1-5271-0740-3

10 9 8 7 6 5 4 3 2 1

Published in 2021
in the
Mentor Imprint
by
Christian Focus Publications Ltd,
Geanies House, Fearn, Ross-shire,
IV20 1TW, Great Britain.

www.christianfocus.com

Cover design by
Daniel van Straaten

Printed and bound by Bell & Bain

# CONTENTS

# LIST OF ABBREVIATIONS

MACCH    Manuscripts of Robert Murray M'Cheyne, New College Library, Edinburgh

*BOF*    *Basket of Fragments*

*CIS*    *Comfort in Sorrow*

*FL*    *Familiar Letters*

*HTD*    *Helps to Devotion*

*MAR*    *Memoir and Remains of Robert Murray M'Cheyne*

*NTS*    *New Testament Sermons*

*OTS*    *Old Testament Sermons*

*SC*    *The Seven Churches of Asia*

*SOH*    *Sermons on Hebrews*

*TBJ*    *The Believer's Joy*

*TPH*    *From the Preacher's Heart*

*TPP*    *The Passionate Preacher*

*WCF*    *Westminster Confession of Faith*

*WLC*    *Westminster Larger Catechism*

*WSC*    *Westminster Shorter Catechism*

'O, if all the pastors of our church, or a large portion of them, were such as M'Cheyne, as dead to the world as he was; as full of sanctified unceasing ardour to do good to the souls of men; as watchful to instruct and edify the young and the old; as much like Christ in all their habits and efforts – what a different aspect would our portion of the religious community wear? How much more elevated would be the eloquence of our pulpits! An eloquence not growing out of the principles and rules of art, but governed and animated by that heart-felt sense of the infinite importance and preciousness of evangelical truth which never fails to reach the heart. How much more frequent would be revivals of religion! ... My hope is, that the great Head of the church will speedily rise up a race of ministers more holy, more zealous, more wise, more diligent, and more entirely devoted to their work than their fathers have ever been.'[1]

---

1. Samuel Miller, 'Introductory Letter,' *Memoir and Remains of the Rev. Robert Murray M'Cheyne*, Andrew A. Bonar (Philadelphia: Paul T. Jones, 1844), pp. xvii-xviii.

# Introduction

IT was Thursday, 21 November 1839. News had spread throughout the city that Robert Murray M'Cheyne was home. The young pastor had been away from his congregation for over six months, traveling on the renowned *Mission of Inquiry* to Palestine.

Thursday evenings were special in the life of St. Peter's, Dundee. In the first year of his ministry at the church, M'Cheyne started a Thursday night prayer service. Over eight hundred souls gathered weekly to storm the throne of grace. The prayerful spirit that pervaded the meetings led him to conclude: 'They would doubtless be remembered in eternity with songs of praise.' A solemn stillness saturated the building until the prayer meeting's final word. The atmosphere of heaven was all around; few ever left hastily for no one wanted 'to get out of God's presence'.[1]

The church was soon overflowing on that evening in 1839. No seat was available. The aisles were full. The pulpit stairs had become pews for the aging and the young. Minds were stirred; hearts were restless. What news would M'Cheyne bring from Palestine? What portraits of grace would he paint of God's work in the Holy Land? But news of the Holy Land, he did not bring. He instead brought the timeless *euangelion* – the good news of salvation in Jesus Christ. He meant to seize the moment for the Savior.

M'Cheyne's return to his pulpit was not the sole reason for his church's palpable excitement. Since August, St. Peter's had been drinking the waters of revival through the ministry of William Chalmers Burns. Meetings were held every night. Dozens of smaller

---

1. Bonar, *MAR*, p. 62.

prayer meetings punctuated each day in Dundee. It was as if God had woken the whole city. M'Cheyne had first heard the news of awakening while in Germany. He had quickly posted a note to Burns: 'You remember it was the prayer of my heart when we parted, that you might be a thousandfold more blessed to the people than ever my ministry had been. How it will gladden my heart, if you can really tell me it has been so!'[2]

Thus, the throbbing excitement energizing St. Peter's that evening was not due merely to M'Cheyne's return; it was also symptomatic of a congregational spirit awakened to spiritual realities.

Prior to their arrival at the church, M'Cheyne and Burns prayed together for increased blessing. They soon entered the church building and ascended the pulpit's sacred steps. M'Cheyne led the church in song, prayed, and turned his attention to 1 Corinthians 2:1-4:

> And I, brethren, when I came to you, came not with excellency of speech or of wisdom, declaring unto you the testimony of God. For I determined not to know anything among you, save Jesus Christ, and him crucified. And I was with you in weakness, and in fear, and in much trembling. And my speech and my preaching was not with enticing words of man's wisdom, but in demonstration of the Spirit and of power (KJV).

He preached on the matter, the manner, and the accomplishments of Paul's preaching. The response was unlike anything he had experienced in Dundee. It was so intense that crowds engulfed M'Cheyne and escorted him back to his house. Sensing the Spirit's work, he preached another short sermon on the street and prayed for the people. Once inside, he closed his door and sighed, 'To thy name, O Lord, to thy name, O Lord, be all the glory.'

## Christ-Centered Piety and Power

If one wants to know the essence of Robert Murray M'Cheyne, his actions on 21 November 1839 provide his ministry in miniature. The characteristic features of his gospel labor are on full display: deep friendships with ministers, revival labors, praying, singing, preaching, and shepherding.

---

2. Ibid., p. 234.

Few figures in church history have left such a long legacy of influence, while not reaching their fourth decade. The popular perception of M'Cheyne is one that concentrates on his holiness. For decades many have summarized his passion with the (almost certainly) apocryphal quote, 'The greatest need of my people is my personal holiness.' He may not have uttered those exact words, but he did often say things that are quite similar. He told a ministerial friend: 'In great measure, according to the purity and perfections of the instrument, will be the success. It is not great talents God blesses so much as great likeness to Jesus. A holy minister is an awful weapon in the hand of God.'[3] The name of 'M'Cheyne' is virtually synonymous with 'personal holiness' – and for good reason.

M'Cheyne's piety has stunned numerous pastors and scholars. L. J. Van Valen, for example, affirms that 'the great secret of M'Cheyne's proclamation is holiness.'[4] Likewise, David Yeaworth says, 'The key to McCheyne's ministerial success lay in his personal holiness and its manifestation to those around him.'[5] A few years after M'Cheyne's death, John Angell James referred to him as 'that seraphic man.'[6] J. W. Alexander, the great pastor-theologian of Princeton Seminary, wrote to a friend: 'The [holy] life of M'Cheyne humbles me. What zeal and faith! What a proof that Old Calvinism is not insusceptible of being used as an arousing instrument!'[7] According to *The Methodist Review*, M'Cheyne was 'a marvel ... of holiness.'[8] In the words of *The Christian Review*, he was a man 'eminently devoted to God.'[9] He was, to Martyn Lloyd-Jones, the 'saintly Robert Murray M'Cheyne.'[10]

M'Cheyne's zeal for godliness shines with unusual radiance, and thus challenges our own struggles for piety. This book seeks to dive even deeper, to the bedrock of his spiritual foundation. Learning from him cannot begin with his pattern of personal holiness. His devotional

---

3. Ibid., p. 282.

4. Van Valen, p. 477.

5. Yeaworth, p. 96.

6. James, *An Earnest Ministry*, p. 120.

7. Quoted in Garretson, p. 210, n. 27.

8. *The Methodist Review* (January 1873), p. 172.

9. Smith, *The Christian Review*, 13:581.

10. Lloyd-Jones, p. 231. See also, Carson, *For the Love of God*, p. 11.

practices do not make sense until we see them as stemming from a more primal spiritual force. If one has eyes to see, there is a much more undeniable pulsebeat in his life and ministry. It is a pulsating power contemporary pastors and Christians must recover as they walk in the path of holiness. That force is *love for Christ*. Love for Christ is what propels a holy ministry and compels a holy minister (2 Cor. 5:14).

*A Holy Minister* aims to recover M'Cheyne's Christ-centered passion by showing how it dominated his life. To focus on the fruits of his *abiding* in Christ runs the risk of missing how, for him, true spiritual life is found only through abiding *in Christ*. So, yes, we want to notice – and we will! – his fruitful pursuit of the Savior. His unrelenting passion for piety convicts our contemporary complacency. His devotion to the means of grace is worth underscoring and underlining. His yearning to save souls humbles our small efforts in evangelism. His longing for eternity is a sharp contrast with our worldliness. But first, we need to see that such fruits flowed from the root of loving communion with Jesus Christ.

The main point of this book is to show *why*, not just how, M'Cheyne understood personal piety as primary in the Christian life (Heb. 12:14). Here is my thesis in a nutshell: M'Cheyne prayed for, preached for, and pursued holiness because he understood it to be the mature expression of love to Christ.

Maturity in Christ is the goal of Christian ministry (Col. 1:28). From one degree to the next, God's Spirit fashions us after Christ's image (2 Cor. 3:18). Such growth only comes through love. In John 15:9-10, Jesus distills the essentials of a Christ-centered life: 'As the Father has loved me, so have I loved you. Abide in my love. If you keep my commandments, you will abide in my love, just as I have kept my Father's commandments and abide in his love.'

## A Specific and Full Portrait

Parts of this book tread on well-worn lanes of study. Many sources have ably detailed the Dundee revival. Others have done careful work on M'Cheyne's missionary zeal. Yet more have explained his practices in Bible reading and prayer. We will walk along those paths too. I want also to underscore elements of his life that are often overlooked or misunderstood.

First, we must know truth not only about his life, but also about those historical forces that influenced him. M'Cheyne lived in an evangelical and cultural moment that produced a stage on which he could shine. Further, he drank from the waters of historical theology, finding heroes in men like Samuel Rutherford, Thomas Boston, and Jonathan Edwards. Contemporaries like Thomas Chalmers and Robert Smith Candlish were notable mentors.

Additionally, there are aspects of M'Cheyne's theology that are sometimes forgotten. He was a man of the Westminster Confession. Two of the famous peculiarities of the Confession, its federal theology and Sabbatarianism, were key features in his ministry. He was a covenant theologian, who grounded his free offer of the gospel in Christ – who is the covenant (Isa. 42:6; 49:8). He was also a soldier for the Sabbath. Some of his most prominent, and polemical, public moments came during what was called 'The Sabbath Railroad Controversy.'

Third, M'Cheyne's grammar of the Christian life came from the Song of Songs. In his candidating sermon at St. Peter's, he declared: 'There is no book of the Bible which affords a better test of the depth of a man's Christianity than the Song of Solomon.'[11] Like most of his contemporaries, he swam in a hermeneutical sea that understood the Song of Songs as a parable of the love between Christ and His church. Nothing better reveals his understanding of holiness as a communion of love between Christ and the believer than his preference for speaking of the means of grace as 'trysts' – meetings between lovers.

These historical, theological, and spiritual factors afford a fuller portrait of M'Cheyne's program for piety.

## About the Sources

M'Cheyne's name is forever linked with that of his great friend Andrew Bonar. The year after M'Cheyne died, Bonar published *The Life of Robert Murray M'Cheyne*. The work was expanded and revised over the years, and it remains in print. Charles Spurgeon told his students at The Pastors' College that Bonar's *Memoir and Remains of Robert Murray M'Cheyne* 'is one of the best and most profitable volumes ever

---

11. Bonar, *MAR*, p. 437.

published. The memoir of such a man ought surely to be in the hands of every Christian and certainly every preacher of the Gospel.'[12] Bonar's book remains the primary sourcebook for M'Cheyne studies. But it is not the only available resource. The ensuing study also engages with the entire catalog of M'Cheyne's writings – sermons, letters, and notebooks archived in the New College, Edinburgh. I have added other textures found in relevant biographies, histories, monographs, and dissertations on matters related to his life and times.

Readers who desire a more detailed academic study may want to consult my previous work, *A Communion of Love: The Christ-Centered Spirituality of Robert Murray M'Cheyne*.[13] The present volume leans on my previous work, but it is a new retelling of an old story.

## A Word to the Pastors

I believe that M'Cheyne's life speaks a sermon to gospel ministers. So, while the ensuing content is no doubt applicable to all Christians, M'Cheyne's model is especially powerful for pastors. If we are to see revival in our time, we need to first see revival in the ministry. We long for the Spirit to give us an army of ministers who proclaim Jesus Christ's unsearchable riches with sincerity and unction. We need men consumed with a passion for Jesus Christ. We need men who are prone to spend long hours on their knees. We need men who are unashamed of the gospel, ready to take it onto every highway and into every byway. We need men who are both tough and tender with God's Word. We need men who exhaust themselves in Christ's labor because they know eternity hangs in the balance – and may call at any time.

The apostle Paul commanded, 'Join in imitating me, and keep your eyes on those who walk according to the example you have in us' (Phil. 3:17). M'Cheyne offers a model of apostolic ministry we need to retrieve. Let us learn from him as we seek to love Christ more.

---

12. C. H. Spurgeon, *Lectures*, p. 70.
13. Jordan Stone, *A Communion of Love*.

# PART 1:
# A Life of Holiness

# CHAPTER 1

# The Life and Times of Robert Murray M'Cheyne

THE year 1813 was a 'golden age' in Scottish history. The Industrial Revolution had expanded commerce and industry. Academics, arts, and sciences flourished in universities and cities. The nation's spiritual climate was undergoing a change as well for the better. Evangelical religion was replacing the old and cold Moderatism that marked the Scottish Church in the late 1700s. Andrew Bonar wrote of the times: 'Eminent men of God appeared to plead the cause of Christ. The cross was being lifted up boldly in the midst of the church courts which had long been ashamed of the gospel of Christ. More spirituality and deeper seriousness began ... to prevail among the youth of our divinity halls. In the midst of such events ... [M'Cheyne] was born.'[1]

## 1813–1831: From Birth to New Birth

Robert Murray M'Cheyne was born in Edinburgh on 21 May 1813, to Adam and Lockhart M'Cheyne.[2] Adam was a lawyer, and the following year he joined the Society of Writers to His Majesty's Signet. This ancient society conducted cases before the Court of Session, the supreme civil court in Scotland. The society Writers also had the exclusive right to prepare crown writs, charters, and precepts. Adam's new position brought increased income and a chance to scale the social ladder,

---

1. Bonar, *MAR*, p. 1.
2. Adam lived from 1781 to 1854 and Lockhart from 1772 to 1854.

moving up from the working class of his family. It was not long before he was noted as a man of social importance, and his home distinguished with goods, furnishings, and ample space.

Adam's personality was direct, and his work ethic disciplined. He was the home's clear authority and he later admitted, 'It was no part of my character to spare the rod.'[3] He trained his children to cherish hard work and learning. While Adam cut a strong – and at times stern – figure, the home was full of life and warmth. This was mostly due to Lockhart's influence on the family.

Like her husband, Lockhart was the youngest child in her family. However, unlike Adam, she entered marriage having known the privilege of belonging to society's upper echelon. Her father 'was the proprietor of the Nether Locharwood estate, the most prosperous in Ruthwell parish.'[4] She was thus accustomed to the comfortable lifestyle that Adam's position as Writer afforded. Her personality complemented his in noticeable ways. She tenderized his demanding nature, creating an environment in which the children were not only accountable, but also cherished. Taken together, Adam and Lockhart trained their children to be self-controlled, studious, and adventurous. The children knew the pleasant routine of schoolwork and play.

Robert was close with both parents. As so often happens, his time with his father sharpened his resolve and courage, while his interactions with his mother fertilized tenderness. His later letters to his family reveal a deeply devoted relationship with his mother. Their kindred spirit could be called 'affectionate,' even 'sentimental,' and solidified a life-long bond.

Adam and Lockhart wed in 1802. They had five children together, with Robert as the youngest. David Thomas (1804–1831) was the firstborn. He followed his father into the legal profession and was counted as 'the pride of his home.'[5] Next came Mary Elizabeth (1806–1888), Robert's constant companion and helper during his time in Dundee. Because she lived with Robert in adulthood and oversaw his domestic affairs, Robert called her 'my own Deaconess and helpmeet.'[6]

---

3. Quoted in Yeaworth, p. 27.
4. Yeaworth, p. 7.
5. Smellie, p. 35.
6. Ibid., p. 22.

William Oswald (1809–1892) was the third child; he studied medicine and eventually went to India with the Bengal Medical Service in 1831. He retired as a surgeon in the Honourable East India Company. Isabella was born in 1811 and died of sickness four months later. Interestingly, none of the M'Cheyne children ever married.

## A Popular Student

By all accounts, a calm ambiance permeated the home of Robert's youth. The siblings were closely knit, and the older children regularly assisted the younger ones in their schoolwork. Adam's occupation provided relaxed living quarters and his esteem for education meant intellectual growth was the children's primary labor. From the start, Robert displayed singular aptitude for learning. Adam recalled how, at the age of four, Robert memorized the Greek alphabet 'as an amusement' while recovering from illness.[7]

In virtually every class during his schooling, Robert was one of the most popular students. He was teachable and capable, attractive and inventive. His form was even distinguished – tall and slender for his age. His favorite childhood pastimes were friends, athletics (particularly gymnastics), poetry, sketching, and achievement. Childhood acquaintances remembered his disposition as equally ambitious and winsome. The Spirit later sanctified these characteristics, which so often war against each other, so that they were driving aspects in his subsequent ministry.

One oft-repeated family legend underscores Robert's competitive streak. After completing the English School with only the second prize, he came home dejected. His older siblings had taken the first prize, after all.

In many ways, Robert's early character manifested a maturity in contrasting traits. He was competitive, yet kind. He was firm, yet patient. He was an artist who happened also to be organized. He loved to sketch rural scenes and portraits of friends. His poetic pen frequently spilled ink onto various pages. His creative streak did not mean he possessed a mind given to flights of fancy. Instead, his

---

7. Van Valen, p. 16.

life exuded discipline and neatness. At the age of sixteen, he wrote an essay titled, 'On Early Rising.' His essential argument was that although 'sleep was necessary for babies and children, there came a time when it was more profitable to curtail the hours in which a man wastes "the best and most useful part of his life in drowsiness and lying in bed."'[8]

M'Cheyne attended the English School from 1818–1821, earning highest marks in recitation and singing. In 1821, he advanced to the High School, where he quickly developed a delight in studying classics and history – 'Virgil, Horace, Ovid, and Tibullus enthralled him; and he did more than the required translations.'[9] In November of 1827, he entered the University of Edinburgh, 'when it was basking in the glory of many outstanding professors, and when science and letters were at their zenith.'[10] His facility in Latin and Greek provided much deeper study in the classics. He left every class with honors, further demonstrating his unique abilities and intellect.

## From Crisis to Christ

The M'Cheynes were devout churchgoers. Yet, most of their religious commitment seemed to be little more than external and formal. In Robert's early years, the family attended the Tron Church in Edinburgh, where Alexander Brunton and William Simpson ministered. Brunton was a force in the Church of Scotland, serving as moderator of the 1832 General Assembly and eventually as Professor of Hebrew and Oriental Languages at the University of Edinburgh. Part of the Church's teaching tradition of the time was that churches typically hosted a children's catechism class between the morning and afternoon services. M'Cheyne devoted himself to the class at the Tron Church and his friends recalled 'his correct and sweet recitation' of Scripture passages and answers to the Shorter Catechism.[11]

In 1829, the M'Cheynes moved to the newly erected St. Stephen's Church. It was a significant move. While the family appears to have

---

8. Yeaworth, p. 15.
9. Ibid., p. 25.
10. Ibid., p. 27.
11. Bonar, *MAR*, p. 2.

exchanged congregations only because St. Stephen's was closer to home, it saw them also exchange a Moderate ministry for one with decidedly Evangelical sympathies under William Muir. Robert served the church wherever he could and engaged in relevant ministry. He also become something of a disciple of Muir's. During the winters of 1829–1830 and 1830–1831, he attended special meetings that Muir hosted in the vestry on Thursday evenings. When Robert began to pursue the gospel ministry, Muir was his endorser.

Such a pursuit, however, was far from Robert's mind in his later teenage years. His external piety was a mask that fooled many ministers and church members. Although Muir spoke glowingly of Robert's 'sound' principles and 'exemplary' conduct,[12] he himself later considered his devotion a 'lifeless morality.'[13] Andrew Bonar remembers how Robert 'regarded these as days of ungodliness – days wherein he cherished a pure morality, but lived in heart a Pharisee.'[14] M'Cheyne's analysis came years after his conversion. Therefore, it would be wrong to think of him as conflicted spiritually. He was, during these years, full of happiness and hope. In time, he explained the joy of his childhood with a verse: 'When the tears that we shed were tears of joy, and the pleasures of home were unmixed with alloy.'[15]

Yet, as he finished his university studies, storm clouds of crisis broke over his peace and leisure. First, in April 1831, his brother William departed for India to join the Bengal Medical Service. The M'Cheynes had so far known relational and geographical closeness during Robert's life. William's venture disrupted the family's harmony and caused much anxiety, especially because the conditions in India were unstable and often life-threatening.

The second crisis was the death of Robert's eldest brother. When William left for India, David lay in the grip of a serious fever. The sickness never abated and eventually it claimed David's life on 8 July 1831. His death smacked Robert with an emotional – and spiritual – blow from which he never recovered. Robert 'had long looked up to

---

12. Quoted in Yeaworth, p. 22.
13. Quoted in Robertson, *Awakening*, p. 34.
14. Bonar, *MAR*, p. 2.
15. M'Cheyne, 'Birthday Ode,' quoted in Yeaworth, p. 41.

[David] as the ideal of all that a true man should be, and his death touched him more deeply than words could well express.'[16]

Robert had a good relationship with all his siblings, but he 'regarded [David] as a youthful idol' and closely watched 'his every action.'[17] Years before his death, David had trusted in Jesus Christ for salvation. His love for Christ was evident to all. His family noticed his keen awareness of eternal realities: heaven was glorious, and hell was terrible. All three siblings could tell of times when David counseled them to close with Christ. David thus became the spiritual engine of the M'Cheyne home – perhaps especially to Robert.

Pouring out his heart's despair, Robert took his pen in hand to write a poem titled, 'In Painting the Miniature Likeness of One Departed.' The final section speaks of David's focus on Christ, and its effect on Robert.

> And oh! recall the look of faith sincere,
> With which that eye would scrutinize the page
> That tells us of offended God appeased
> By awful sacrifice upon the cross
> Of Calvary – that bids us leave a world
> Immersed in darkness and in death, and seek
> A better country. Ah! how oft that eye
> Would turn on me, with pity's tenderest look,
> And only half-upbraiding, bid me flee
> From the vain idols of my boyish heart![18]

Early in his ministry, Robert wrote a letter to a young boy in his parish that he did not know well. The child evidently reflected much of Robert's youth. The letter is an insightful window into the young minister's self-evaluation. He thought the parish boy lacked a counselor, which summoned David to Robert's mind:

> I had a kind brother as you have, who taught me many things. He gave me a Bible, and persuaded me to read it; he tried to train me as a gardener trains the apple-tree upon the wall; but all in vain. I thought myself far wiser than he, and would always take my own way; and many a time, I well remember,

---

16. Loane, p. 141.

17. Yeaworth, p. 42.

18. MACCH 1.13.

> I have seen him reading his Bible, or shutting his closet door to pray, when I have been dressing to go to some frolic, or some dance of folly.[19]

David's death made a greater impression on Robert than his life ever did. The loss of his brother was catalytic in Robert's conversion to Christ. While the timing of his turn from sin to the Savior is unclear, there can be no doubt that he 'looked upon the death of his eldest brother, David, as the event which awoke him from the sleep of nature, and brought in the first beam of light to his soul.'[20] Robert's father admitted as much in a letter to Andrew Bonar: 'The holy example and the happy death of his brother David seem by the blessing of God to have given a new impulse to his mind in the right direction.'[21]

Robert himself saw David's loss as a spur to repent of his sin and turn to Christ. On the eleventh anniversary of losing his brother, he wrote: 'This day eleven years ago, I lost my loved and loving brother, and began to seek a Brother who cannot die.'[22]

The spiritual crisis descended on Robert so suddenly that he had no guide at the start of his pilgrim journey. He told a young parishioner:

> This dear friend and brother died; and though his death made a greater impression upon me than ever his life had done, still I found the misery of being *friendless*. I do not mean that I had no relations and worldly friends, for I had many; but I had no friend *who cared for my soul*. I had none to direct me to the Saviour – none to awaken my slumbering conscience – none to tell me about the blood of Jesus washing away all my sin – to change the heart, and give the victory over passions. I had no minister to take me by the hand, and say, 'Come with me, and we will do thee good.'[23]

With no living counselor immediately available, M'Cheyne found help from books. He started reading *The Sum of Saving Knowledge*, a short theological work typically appended to the Westminster Confession of Faith. Andrew Bonar believed the book 'brought him

---

19. Bonar, *MAR*, p. 46.
20. Ibid., p. 4.
21. Quoted in Yeaworth, p. 46.
22. Bonar, *MAR*, p. 9.
23. Ibid., p. 47 (emphasis original).

to a clear understanding of the way of acceptance with God.'[24] Robert penned in his diary years later: 'Read in *The Sum of Saving Knowledge*, the work which I think first of all wrought a saving change in me.'[25] That such a book could bring a soul to assurance fascinated the *British and Foreign Evangelical Review*. The magazine commented years later: 'The Holy Spirit, no doubt, is sovereign in the use of the means which He blesses for conversion; but it is difficult to imagine anything more unlike the style of McCheyne's preaching than the cold and stiff dialectics of that *summa theologiae*.'[26] Even though *The Sum of Saving Knowledge* lacked prose that belong to page-turners of truth, it masters the basic elements of the truth, as it is found in Jesus Christ. Such doctrine was the sound instruction Robert needed at this most-formative stage.

Now assured of God's love, he plunged into Christian service. A spiritual fervor suffused all his labors. Collecting a memory from Adam M'Cheyne, Bonar recalls how Robert's 'poetry was pervaded with serious thought, and all his pursuits began to be followed out in another spirit. He engaged in the labours of a Sabbath school, and began to seek God to his soul, in the diligent reading of the Word, and attendance on a faithful ministry.'[27]

M'Cheyne kept a regular journal of his spiritual experience. The entries made after his conversion present a zeal for holiness reaching down to every part of his life. His was the passion of a new convert: 'I hope never to play cards again'; 'Never visit on a Sunday evening again'; 'Absented myself from the dance; upbraidings ill to bear. But I must try to bear the cross.'[28]

## 1831–1835: Training for Gospel Ministry

The Lord called Robert to ministry almost immediately after calling him to Christ. David 'used to speak of the ministry as the most blessed work on earth, and often expressed the greatest delight in the hope that his

---

24. Ibid., p. 11.
25. Ibid., p. 11.
26. Quoted in Yeaworth, p. 47, n. 4.
27. Bonar, *MAR*, p. 8.
28. Ibid., p. 10.

younger brother might one day become a minister of Christ.'[29] The elder brother's desire was realized on 28 September 1831 when Robert stood before the Presbytery of Edinburgh. The purpose of his appearance was twofold. First, it represented his formal expression of intent to study for the gospel ministry, which he would do at the Divinity Hall at the University of Edinburgh. Second, the Presbytery needed to examine him in the relevant areas before he could proceed. After passing the Presbytery's necessary queries, he received its blessing to enroll as a ministerial student.

Robert started classes six weeks later, at a time when the Divinity Hall was at a zenith point. The student body showed enormous promise, and a venerable party of professors stood ready to train them. The most prominent faculty member was Thomas Chalmers, who 'was at the height of his amazing influence; no one since the days of John Knox had been held in such deep veneration.'[30] Chalmers' divinity lectures riveted ordinary citizens as well as theological students. So much so, in fact, that an extra gallery was built to accommodate the masses.

As Professor of Divinity, Chalmers was responsible for the theology courses. His doctrinal emphases seeped into M'Cheyne's mind, as they did with scores of students. What Chalmers especially etched on Robert's heart, however, was a particular model of ministry that he soon came to personify and exemplify.

Alexander Brunton, M'Cheyne's former minister, was Professor of Hebrew. Robert's affinity for the Old Testament's original language was noticeable. He entered the Divinity Hall with a native ability for languages, and he had already taken a private Hebrew class before enrolling. Thus, for him, the Hebrew lessons were not nearly as difficult as they were for other students. He relished his lessons, recording in his diary one day, 'Hebrew class – Psalms. New beauty in the original every time I read.'[31]

David Welsh, Professor of Ecclesiastical History, was the Divinity Hall's third professor. His exhaustive historical knowledge and exacting

---

29. Ibid., p. 11.
30. Loane, p. 142.
31. Bonar, *MAR*, p. 13.

lectures appealed to M'Cheyne. The young student later confessed he had an ambition to write a history of the German Reformation. Like Chalmers, Welsh also had a spiritual influence on him. What struck Robert most was Welsh's sincere piety and desire to serve his students. His desire to mentor students is seen in a series of private resolutions he set. Several relate to training students for ministry. Two such commitments were 'to set apart one hour *every* Saturday for prayer for my students,' and 'in looking at a student, ask, how can I do him good, or have I ever done him good?'[32]

The Divinity Hall's environment was fertile ground for M'Cheyne's growing passion for Christian ministry. The academic rigor appealed to his expansive intellect. The pietistic passion stirred in him a desire for holiness and panting for Scripture. The faculty's sincere love for Christ struck a chord with Robert and catalyzed a Christ-centered ardor that consumed his spirituality.

The faculty was not the only relational influence on M'Cheyne during those days – there were also several vital friendships.

## Friends and Activity

If there is such a thing as a spiritual gift of friendship, M'Cheyne possessed it. He connected with people from all walks of life. His winsomeness and warmth attracted no small number of confidants and acquaintances.

Two friends at the Divinity Hall were uniquely significant for him: Alexander Somerville and Andrew Bonar. Somerville had been Robert's best friend since High School. Their spiritual experiences were similar, and they began ministerial studies at the same time. Somerville's biographer recalls how 'the two boys passed from school to college in November 1827, and through the Arts classes, foremost in athletic sports, in dancing, and in youthful frolic. Both were handsome and accomplished in the social graces, were great favourites with their fellows, and were inseparable companions.'[33] Another recalled how M'Cheyne and Somerville

---

32. Dunlop, pp. 56-57 (emphasis original).
33. Smith, *A Modern Apostle*, p. 6.

seemed literally inseparable; along with many others I was often amused at the closeness of their companionship. They sat beside each other in the classroom; they came and went together; they were usually seen walking side by side in the street; or if one of them turned round a corner, the other was sure to come a minute after. The one seemed to haunt the other like a shadow, and nothing, apparently, could separate the two friends.[34]

The pair quickly joined the Visiting Society at the Divinity Hall, which aimed 'to set apart an hour or two every week for visiting the careless and needy in the most neglected portions of the town.'[35] M'Cheyne and Somerville concentrated on a district in the Canongate, teaching a Sunday school class and distributing the *Monthly Visitor*, a denominational tract. During his first year, M'Cheyne also joined 'The Exegetical Society,' an exclusive creation of Thomas Chalmers. The Society was 'select in point of membership,' because Chalmers wanted 'none but the very *elite* of the Hall for taste and skill in the languages.'[36] Members gathered every Saturday at 6:30 a.m. to present exegetical papers and interact with the interpretations. Far from hosting only academic argument, the group fostered theological and spiritual growth. The Society members that remained in town during the summer holiday continued to meet once a week. One added element of the summer meetings was that each member shared the 'amount and result' of their private Bible reading.[37]

The Society's roll had sixteen names, and none became more precious to M'Cheyne than its secretary: Andrew Bonar. Bonar was almost three years older than Robert, but he entered the Divinity Hall at the same time. In Bonar, M'Cheyne found a kindred ministerial and devotional spirit. Throughout their days at the Divinity Hall, M'Cheyne, Bonar and Somerville could be found studying together and caring for each other's souls. For example, Bonar wrote in his diary on 30 May 1835: 'In a walk round Duddingston Loch with Robert M'Cheyne and Alexander Somerville this afternoon, we had much conversation upon the leading

34. Quoted in Smith, p. 12.
35. Bonar, *MAR*, p. 22.
36. Yeaworth, p. 71 (emphasis original).
37. Bonar, *MAR*, p. 27.

of Providence and future days. We sang together, sitting upon a fallen oak-tree, one of the Psalms.'[38]

## Spiritual and Ministerial Developments

Theological study did not stunt M'Cheyne's spirituality – the opposite was true. His Divinity Hall studies fanned into flame a fire of Christ-centered piety that no hardships could smother. His diary entries from the Divinity Hall years yearn for more devotion to Christ:

> What right have I to steal and abuse my Master's time? 'Redeem it,' He is crying to me.[39]

> Not a trait worth remembering! And yet these four-and-twenty hours must be accounted for.[40]

> Oh that heart and understanding may grow together, like brother and sister, leaning on one another![41]

> Oh for true, unfeigned humility![42]

> More abundant longings for the work of the ministry. Oh that Christ would but count me faithful, that a dispensation of the gospel might be committed to me![43]

The desired 'dispensation' came in time. On 16 February 1835, one month before completing his divinity studies, M'Cheyne underwent the initial trials for licensure to preach the gospel in the Presbytery of Edinburgh. His mind at the time was equal parts anxiousness and eagerness. He wrote the night before his trials: 'To-morrow I undergo my trials before the Presbytery. May God give me courage in the hour of need. What should I fear? If God see meet to put me into the ministry, who shall keep me back? If I be not meet, why should I be thrust forward? To thy service I desire to dedicate myself over and over again.'[44]

---

38. Marjory Bonar, *Diary and Letters*, p. 27.
39. Bonar, *MAR*, p. 12.
40. Ibid., p. 12.
41. Ibid., p. 16.
42. Ibid., p. 17.
43. Ibid., p. 17.
44. Ibid., p. 26.

The tests covered New Testament Greek, Church History, and Systematic Theology. M'Cheyne left the exams unsure of his success. He told his brother William that the examiners 'all heckled me, like so many terriers on a rat.'[45] His mother quickly heard some inside information that assuaged the family's stress, reporting, 'Dr. Chalmers was highly pleased, and all the other ministers.'[46]

Several ministers promptly invited M'Cheyne to serve as their assistant. The standout offer came from John Bonar, minister at Larbert and Dunipace. Bonar's assistantship was considered particularly attractive. He was a careful mentor and the united parish of Larbert and Dunipace provided immense opportunity to grow in the various parts of gospel ministry. Leaders and friends alike advised M'Cheyne to take Bonar's call. The young student accepted. Because it seemed Edinburgh Presbytery would not examine him until the following year, he applied to Annan Presbytery to complete his trials sooner.

On 1 July 1835, M'Cheyne submitted five different assignments: (1) a Hebrew translation and analysis from Psalm 109; (2) a lecture on Matthew 11:1-15; (3) a homily on Matthew 7:13-14; (4) a concise commentary on Romans 3:27-28; and (5) a sermon on Romans 5:11.[47] He passed each exam and was subsequently licensed to preach the gospel. He wrote in his diary:

> Preached three probationary discourses in Annan Church, and, after an examination in Hebrew, was solemnly licensed to preach the gospel by Mr. Monylaws, the moderator …. What I have so long desired as the highest honour of man, Thou at length givest me – me who dare scarcely use the words of Paul: 'Unto me who am less than the least of all the saints is this grace given, that I should preach the unsearchable riches of Christ.' Felt somewhat solemnized, though unable to feel my unworthiness as I ought. Be clothed with humility.[48]

M'Cheyne's call to Larbert and Dunipace did not take effect until 7 November 1835. In the months leading to his installation, he preached

---

45. Quoted in Smellie, p. 43.
46. Ibid., p. 43.
47. Yeaworth, p. 79, n. 1.
48. Bonar, *MAR*, p. 31.

as a licentiate for the first time in Henry Duncan's Ruthwell Church (where his mother's family lived and M'Cheyne often visited in his youth). The solemnity he felt was absent upon licensure fell when he ascended to the sacred desk in Ruthwell. He wrote that Sabbath evening: 'Found it a more awfully solemn thing than I had imagined to announce Christ authoritatively; yet a glorious privilege!'[49]

## 1835–1843: A Laborer in the Harvest Field

In accepting the call to assist John Bonar, M'Cheyne confessed, 'It has always been my aim, and it is my prayer, to have *no plans* with regard to myself, well assured as I am, that the place where the Saviour sees meet to place me must ever be the best place for me.'[50] In God's providence, serving with Bonar at Larbert and Dunipace proved to be 'the best place.' His first charge established many of the vital elements of gospel ministry that would soon be needed in Dundee. 'Here the groundwork was laid for his future greatness in the pastoral ministry,' comments one admirer.[51]

### Larbert and Dunipace

Six thousand souls populated the united parish of Larbert and Dunipace. The two towns were strikingly different. Larbert was loud, grimy, and full of industrial strength, inhabited primarily by those who worked in coal or iron. Dunipace lay some three miles to the northwest and was a rural abode for shepherds and small farmers.

M'Cheyne and Bonar both preached on the Lord's Day; one in Larbert and the other in Dunipace. A primary feature of their parish ministry was exhaustive visitation throughout the week. Robert found pleasure in the work, telling his mother that it was his favorite aspect of ministry under Bonar.

There were also five preaching stations around Larbert. Such a station represented a regularly gathering congregation, under the leadership of the Presbytery, but without an installed pastor. The

---

49. Ibid., p. 32.
50. Ibid., p. 32 (emphasis original).
51. Loane, p. 147.

number of preaching possibilities gave M'Cheyne great experience for his future pulpit ministry. He preached three times on the Lord's Day and several more times during the week at special Bible classes or meetings. His earliest sermons were simple and evangelistic. While earnest, they do not reflect the depth of feeling that earned eventual acclaim. Congregants listened appreciatively, if not expectedly. Their thankfulness was likely because M'Cheyne rarely preached longer then thirty-five minutes, while Bonar often exceeded ninety minutes.

Sickness, a constant companion through Robert's life, disrupted his ministry in December of 1835, just weeks after he began parish work. 'A doctor diagnosed the beginnings of tuberculosis and determined that his right lung hardly functioned.'[52] He always sought to discover God's providence amidst the affliction; he believed his continued struggle with illness was his Father's discipline, and this occasion was God's chastisement for being 'too anxious to do great things.'[53] Instead of achieving renown, he needed to learn the primacy of prayer – particularly intercessory prayer. He told John Bonar: 'I feel distinctly that the whole of my labour during this season of sickness and pain should be in the way of prayer and *intercession*.'[54]

Illness again set him aside for an extended time several months later. He believed the setback was meant to teach a few spiritual lessons. First, he remarked, 'Set by once more for a season to feel my unprofitableness and cure my pride.' Second, he thought that God meant for the illness to humble his ministerial ambitions. 'The Lord saw I would have spoken as much for my own honour as His, and therefore shut my mouth,' he confessed. '*I see a man cannot be a faithful minister, until he preaches Christ for Christ's sake* – until he gives up striving to attract people to himself, and seeks only to attract them to Christ. Lord, give me this!'[55]

M'Cheyne genuinely enjoyed ministry in Larbert and Dunipace. He nonetheless expressed to his father a desire for increased responsibility: 'My own inclination is to sit still until God see fit to call me somewhere. If not, I am well employed here – and indeed have as much to do as I

---

52. Beaty, p. 17.
53. Bonar, *MAR*, p. 36.
54. Ibid., p. 36 (emphasis original).
55. Ibid., p. 43 (emphasis original).

have strength for. At the same time, I sometimes feel the lack of not having the full powers of a minister of God, for that reason alone I would desire an exchange.'[56] Within a few weeks, the possibility of an exchange arrived. St. Peter's Dundee invited M'Cheyne to preach as a candidate for their first ministerial position.

St. Peter's was a new congregation, started under the guidance of a local pastor named John Roxburgh, who ministered at St. John's. The St. John's session asked Thomas Chalmers, David Welsh and Robert Candlish to provide six names worthy for St. Peter's consideration. They asked for pious, hard-working, and fruitful preachers. The evangelical leaders suggested M'Cheyne, Andrew Bonar, Thomas Dymock, James Gibson, Alexander Somerville, and a Mr. White.[57] Robert Candlish, the eminent minister of St. George's in Edinburgh, 'particularly favored McCheyne' for the St. Peter's position and even tried to secure the most opportune preaching date.[58]

The search process gave M'Cheyne a few reasons for concern. He remarked, 'My two greatest intimates [are] made my rivals. I have no doubt we will be content with all humility in honour preferring one another.'[59] He thought Bonar was the best choice, explaining, 'If the people have any sense, they will choose Andrew Bonar who, for learning, experimental knowledge, and all the valuable qualities of a minister, outstrips all the students I ever knew.'[60] While M'Cheyne sensed the potential relational strain and envy, more significant was the conflict he sensed over where he would best serve Christ. He wrote to his parents: 'If I were to choose the scene of my labours, I would wish to be away from a town – as riding and country air seem almost essential to my existence.'[61] Yet, he believed God's call, through a congregation, was authoritative. Thus, if St. Peter's called, he would go speedily to the post.

Once all six candidates had preached at St. Peter's, the church convened a meeting to pare down the names. It became clear that 'there

---

56. MACCH 2.6.27.
57. Yeaworth, p. 92. There is no record of Mr White's first name.
58. Ibid., p. 92.
59. Ibid., p. 92.
60. Smellie, p. 53.
61. Yeaworth, p. 92.

was so decided a preference for McCheyne that a motion was made to dispense with any further hearings. This was carried by a large majority, and the minority agreed to make it unanimous.'[62] He thus became the first minister in St. Peter's history.

Robert proceeded to close out his ministry at Larbert and Dunipace. He was thrilled to hear that Alexander Somerville would succeed him as John Bonar's assistant. M'Cheyne's self-examination on his time under Bonar was less than self-congratulatory. He wrote to his family after preaching for the last time in Dunipace:

> I never saw the church so full before. … It is very sad to leave them now and to leave them thus. What multitudes of houses I have never entered. So many I have only stood once on their hearthstone – and prayed. In some few I have found my way so far into their affections – but not so far as to lead them to Jesus. My classes are a little more anxious and awakened than they were – especially some of the young men; but permanent fruit – none is visible. Yet I leave them just as the farmer leaves the seed he has sown. It is not the farmer that can make it grow – he can only pray and wait for the … latter rain.[63]

He exhorted Somerville to improve on his efforts, writing: 'Take more heed to the saints than I ever did …. Speak boldly, what matters in eternity the slight awkwardnesses of time?'[64]

Although M'Cheyne may not have considered his time in Larbert and Dunipace effective, Andrew Bonar argued that it laid the foundation for his success in Dundee:

> During these ten months the Lord had done much for him, but it was chiefly in the way of discipline for a future ministry. He had been taught a minister's heart; he had been tried in the furnace; he had tasted deep personal sorrow, little of which has been recorded; he had felt the fiery darts of temptation; he had been exercised in self-examination and in much prayer; he had proved how flinty is the rock, and had learnt that in lifting the rod by which it was to be smitten, success lay in Him alone who enabled him to lift it up. And thus prepared of God for the peculiar work that awaited him, he had turned his face towards Dundee.[65]

---

62. Ibid., p. 93.
63. Quoted in Yeaworth, pp. 93-94.
64. Quoted in Smith, *A Modern Apostle*, p. 20.
65. Bonar, *MAR*, p. 51.

M'Cheyne's ministry in Dundee would divide into two three-year segments, with a journey to Jerusalem in the middle. The first three years were primarily years of sowing the gospel seed. The final three years reaped the harvest.

## Ministry at St. Peter's

When M'Cheyne arrived at St. Peter's in 1836, the city was a center of bustling industry. Roughly 3,400 people resided within the parish boundaries, the vast majority of whom never entered a church building. He expected the labor to be intense and full of spiritual battle. He believed the city was 'given to idolatry and hardness of heart. I fear there is much of what Isaiah speaks of: "The prophets prophesy lies, and the people love to have it so."'[66]

M'Cheyne was ordained to the gospel ministry on 24 November 1836. The next Lord's Day he preached his first sermon at St. Peter's from Isaiah 61:1-3, focusing on verse 1: 'The Spirit of the Lord GOD is upon me; because the LORD hath anointed me to preach good tidings unto the meek; he hath sent me to bind up the brokenhearted, to proclaim liberty to the captives, and the opening of the prison to them that are bound (KJV).' He returned to this same text every year on the anniversary of his first Sabbath as pastor.

Robert's vitality energized St. Peter's. He preached three times each Lord's Day, and the thousand-seat building overflowed with congregants. He soon installed ten elders to the church session. He began a Thursday night prayer meeting that bulged with eight hundred participants. During the summer months, he held weekly 'meetings for singing,' which he designed to increase the congregation's skill in song. He also increased the number of annual communion seasons from two to four – a novelty for the time. His special interest in shepherding young souls led him to create a Sabbath school for children, and a Tuesday evening catechism class for students. Some two hundred and fifty young people attended the latter class.

His commitment to Presbyterian polity made him a noticeable figure in the courts of the Church. He became the Secretary for Church Extension

---

66. Ibid., p. 57.

in 1837. The following year's General Assembly appointed a committee 'to ascertain the numbers, condition and character of the Jewish people in Palestine and Europe; to discover what means had been previously employed for their spiritual good, and the success of such enterprises; and to seek possible locations for mission stations.' M'Cheyne was added to the committee, and he engaged in the work zealously because he believed God still had a plan for 'his peculiar people.'

His growing prominence made him a prime candidate for other churches looking for a minister. In 1837, Sir Thomas Carmichael asked M'Cheyne to lead the church in the parish of Skirling. It was a tempting offer. The position offered a substantial increase in salary. The parish was also substantially smaller than his current charge, numbering only three hundred souls. Skirling's rural setting was also better suited to his personality – and health. Nonetheless, he refused the offer. He told his parents: 'You cannot imagine – unless you know how rural my tastes are – how suitable to my nature this change would have been. And yet God has seen fit to place me here among the bustling artisans and political manufacturers of Dundee. Perhaps He will make this wilderness of chimney tops to be green and beautiful as the garden of the Lord.'[67]

He felt obliged to explain to Lady Carmichael his reasoning for declining the call. At the root of the matter was his trust that God sovereignly placed him at St. Peters. Thus to leave the congregation so soon after starting would be to relinquish a divine mandate and opportunity. 'I am here (in Dundee), I did not bring myself here,' he wrote. 'I did not ask to be made a candidate for this place. I was hardly willing to be a candidate. I was as happy at Larbert as the day was long. And yet God has turned the hearts of this whole people towards me like the heart of one man.'[68]

Robert's mother, in particular, agonized over her son's decision to remain in Dundee. She had quickly concluded that long-term ministry there was not probable for him. The environs of Dundee would, she thought, plague his health and lead to an early death. Why would he not leave for Skirling, which ensured a long-lasting ministry for Christ?

---

67. Quoted in Yeaworth, p. 188.
68. MACCH 2.1.6.

Robert initially tried writing to his father, asking him to calm Lockhart's fear. Yet her pen persisted in pleading with Robert, via letters, to take the call in Skirling. After a few days of back and forth, Robert wrote more forcefully:

> Dear Mamma, you must just make up your mind to let me be murdered among the lanes of Dundee – instead of seeing me fattening in the green plebe of Skirling. Perhaps it would have been very good for my frail body Dear Mamma – but then I fear my soul would have turned sickly. I would have felt myself a renegade. I never had a shade of doubt that I would refuse. Dear Mamma, be content and be happy, we are only pilgrims – we shall soon be in the land of plenty.[69]

Little did Robert know that a most unexpected, and altogether different, pilgrimage awaited: a journey to the Holy Land.

## The Mission of Inquiry

The Church's committee on missions to the Jews consisted of one hundred members. They possessed full power to execute their task: discovering the current state of missionary endeavors and discerning possible locations for future mission works. Initially, they accrued data through correspondence with influential individuals – missionaries and public officials. It soon became clear, however, that on-the-ground knowledge was necessary. Thus, it was decided that a small deputation should travel to Palestine and deliver a report on their experience. The team was due to leave in 1839.

In late 1838, heart palpitations forced M'Cheyne to recoup at his parents' home in Edinburgh. Robert Candlish visited him while he recovered. Candlish, who at that time was the eminent preacher of Scotland's capital, thought Robert should join the deputation to Palestine, because the change in climate would aid his health. After praying and consulting with other leaders, M'Cheyne agreed and was added to the team. The other members were Alexander Black, Professor of Divinity at Marischal College, Aberdeen; Alexander Keith, minister at St. Cyrus; Robert Wodrow, a ruling elder in Glasgow (illness ultimately prevented him from going), and Andrew Bonar joined him on the mission.

---

69. MACCH 2.1.8.

M'Cheyne was the first team member to depart. On 27 March 1839, he traveled to London to make the necessary preparations for the trip to Palestine. He also spent two weeks urging English churches to support the mission. The Mission of Inquiry set sail on 12 April. Their journey took them first to France, then to Egypt by steam ship, and then to Palestine by camel. On 7 June, they arrived in Jerusalem. M'Cheyne described the day as 'one of the most privileged' of his life.[70] As he looked over David's city, he recorded: 'Soon, all of us were on the spot, buried in thought, and wistfully gazing on the wondrous scene where the Redeemer died. The nearer we came to the city, the more we felt it a solemn thing to be where "God manifest in the flesh" had walked. The feelings of that hour could not even be spoken. We all moved forward in silence, or interchanging feelings only by a word.'[71]

After several days in the City of Peace, the deputation split into two groups because of Black's ill health. Black and Keith returned home via Constantinople, while M'Cheyne and Bonar remained in Palestine. The friends spent the extra time logging various observations deemed vital to future mission work. They returned home by way of Bosphorus, Moldavia, Wallachia, and Poland. Difficulty seemed to haunt their pathway home – especially in Poland. One biographer recalls how, 'Being contrary to Roman Catholic doctrine, [Bonar and M'Cheyne's] books were confiscated, and every movement was followed with "inquisitorial suspicion." M'Cheyne was also attacked bodily by two shepherds as he read in an open field, being left only as he lay helpless on the ground after a bitter struggle.'[72] Quickly healed, M'Cheyne and Bonar pressed homeward with renewed vigor.

The deputies arrived in London on 6 November to great acclaim. They soon found themselves preaching in congregations throughout the United Kingdom, recounting their journey and soliciting funds for additional missions to the Jews. At the 1840 General Assembly, Keith assisted M'Cheyne in submitting the mission's final report. That same year, M'Cheyne and Bonar set to work on publishing their *Narrative*

---

70. M'Cheyne, *Familiar Letters,* p. 98.
71. Quoted in Prime, pp. 82-83.
72. Yeaworth, pp. 271-72.

*of a Mission of Inquiry to the Jews from the Church of Scotland in 1839.*
Once published, the work received extensive praise. 'I have the greatest
value for it,' Chalmers admitted.[73] The Church of Scotland encouraged
ministers to read the book at prayer meetings, offer it as a prize to
children, and include it in parish libraries.

As if the mission's success was not sufficient cause for thanksgiving
to God, M'Cheyne also returned home and saw St. Peter's was in the
midst of revival.

## Revival Preacher

Before leaving for Palestine, M'Cheyne wrote: 'I sometimes think that
a great blessing may come to my people in my absence. Often God does
not bless us in the midst of our labours, lest we shall say, "My hand and
eloquence have done it." He removes us into silence, and then pours
down a blessing so there is no room to receive it; so that all that see it
cry out, "It is the Lord!"'[74] His words proved prophetic.

In February 1839, M'Cheyne asked Alexander Somerville to approach
William Chalmers Burns about filling St. Peter's pulpit while the deputation
traveled to and from Palestine. Although Burns was only twenty-three
years old, he had some renown as a preacher of unusual power. Burns
was interested in the interim work, but there was an immediate hurdle:
he was already committed to missionary service in India. He could not
guarantee the lengthy assistance that M'Cheyne required. The Colonial
Committee settled the matter speedily, though, by reminding Burns that
no missionary openings were currently available. Burns thus agreed to
M'Cheyne's request and commenced preaching at St. Peter's.

From April to late July, Burns preached with little noticeable effect
on the congregation. At the end of July, he had to travel to Paisley for
his brother-in-law's funeral. The memorial service impressed on him
the urgency of eternity. He then traveled to Kilsyth to assist his father
in the parish's communion season. It was there that he brought 'that
hidden fire which at Paisley was roused into a flame.'[75] He preached a few
more times during the communion week and the Spirit seemed ready to

---

73. Smellie, p. 83.
74. Bonar, *MAR*, p. 86.
75. Quoted in Yeaworth, p. 290.

enflame countless souls. The following Tuesday, he preached from Psalm 110:3: 'Thy people shall be willing in the day of thy power (KJV).' The sermon generated throbbing emotional outbursts and thus the famous Kilsyth Revival was born. It continued at full power for three months. One observer recounted the breadth of spiritual awakening:

> The web became nothing to the weaver, nor the forge to the blacksmith, nor his bench to the carpenter, nor his furrow to the ploughman. They forsook all to crowd the churches and the prayer-meetings. There were nightly sermons in every church, household meetings for prayer in every street, twos and threes in earnest conversation on every road, and single wrestlers with God in the solitary places of the field and glen.[76]

Burns returned to Dundee on Thursday, 8 August. M'Cheyne lay flat on his bed that very day, suffering from sickness. The Spirit moved him to intercede for his flock at St. Peter's.

Burns led the Thursday prayer meeting as usual. He told of the Lord reviving Kilsyth. He invited anyone to remain 'who felt the need of an outpouring of the Spirit to convert them.'[77] One hundred souls stayed in the room. Burns spoke to them on the need for immediate conversion to Christ. By the end of his message 'the power of God seemed to descend, and all were bathed in tears.'[78] A similar service was held the following night with comparable results. From then on, meetings were held nightly. The Spirit seemed to have revived the entire city.

M'Cheyne first heard of the awakening while in Hamburg. He promptly posted a note to Burns, saying: 'You remember it was the prayer of my heart when we parted, that you might be a thousandfold more blessed to the people than ever my ministry had been. How it will gladden my heart, if you can really tell me it has been so!'[79] He soon found it was indeed so.

His first public meeting in Dundee, after returning from Palestine, was at the Thursday night prayer meeting on 21 November. An enormous, standing-room-only crowd filled the building, eager to

---

76. Quoted in Prime, p. 96.
77. Bonar, *MAR*, p. 114.
78. Ibid., p. 114.
79. Ibid., p. 234.

hear about the mission to Palestine. Yet, M'Cheyne sensed a new spirit among the people. Instead of providing a report, he preached from 1 Corinthians 2:1-4. The response was immediate and something he had not yet seen in Dundee. He told his parents: 'I never preached to such an audience, so many weeping, so many waiting for the words of eternal life. I never heard such sweet singing anywhere, so tender and affecting, as if the people felt that they were praising a present God.'[80] Congregants were unable to restrain their emotions as the Holy Spirit moved. Bonar recalled, 'On one occasion, for instance, when [M'Cheyne] was speaking tenderly on the words, "He is altogether lovely," almost every sentence was responded to by cries of the bitterest agony.'[81]

Burns continued co-laboring with M'Cheyne for several weeks. Robert saw special gifts in Burns: 'His views of Divine truth are clear and commanding. There is a great deal of substance in what he preaches, and his manner is very powerful – so much so that he sometimes made me tremble. In private, he is deeply prayerful, and seems to feel his danger of falling into pride.'[82]

During those final months of 1839, some six hundred to seven hundred people conversed with the ministers about their spiritual state. The revival continued through the spring of 1840, spreading into nearby areas as M'Cheyne and Burns itinerated. The spiritual fire started dwindling by July of 1840. Robert noted how few were crying out for conversion. He lamented that too many had let the revival spirit pass by without them being saved, yet he rejoiced that he could only count two people who had 'openly given the lie to their profession.'[83]

## Final Years

Praying, preaching, and visiting continued to mark M'Cheyne in the last years of his life and ministry. There was, however, a new practice that preoccupied him: itinerant preaching.

His pulpit renown only increased after the *Mission of Inquiry*, and soon he had numerous occasions to preach Christ outside of Dundee.

---

80. Smellie, p. 139.
81. Bonar, *MAR*, p. 501.
82. Ibid., p. 118.
83. Ibid., p. 497.

He traveled extensively throughout Scotland, visited Belfast on two occasions, and, in 1842, contributed to what he called 'a preaching raid into England.'[84] His success as an evangelist caused William Burns to urge full-time itinerant ministry:

> Oh! that you and a few more of our brethren were cast forth by the Lord to the field in which I am favoured to be. The people are waiting in the market place until someone call them in the name of Jesus. ... I often wish I were laboring along with you from place to place. ... Why should St. Peter's or any other parish have shower upon shower when many districts have not a drop! The time is short. Come away to the help of the Lord.[85]

M'Cheyne's preference at the time was to indeed 'come away' to the fields of evangelistic ministry. 'I think God will yet make me a wandering minister. My nature inclines thereto,' he admitted to his sister.[86] His traveling ministry continued into the spring of 1843. In February, he traveled on his final evangelistic tour in the districts of Deer and Ellon, preaching twenty-four times over three weeks.

He came home to Dundee on 1 March. Typhus fever raged in the parish, but it did not stop M'Cheyne from his typical visitation scheme. The northern trip from which he returned had left him exhausted and weakened. Unsurprisingly, he soon complained of symptoms that led to the diagnosis, 'You have the typhus fever.'

News spread throughout the city that he lay near death. The lane leading to his home overflowed with concerned parishioners. St. Peter's was full every night with people praying for God to intervene.

M'Cheyne was well enough to deliver what proved to be his final sermon on Sunday, 12 March. He preached in the morning on Hebrew 9:15 'with uncommon solemnity,' and on Romans 9:22-23 in the afternoon 'with peculiar strength upon the sovereignty of God.'[87]

Forty-eight hours later, Robert was in the typhus fever's death grip. The doctor confined him to his bed, and family members filled the room as his health continually declined. He cried out words of exhortation

---

84. Quoted in Yeaworth, p. 300.
85. Ibid., p. 300.
86. Ibid., p. 301.
87. Bonar, *MAR*, p. 162.

and intercession at various points in his delirium. In one such moment, he shouted suddenly, 'This parish, Lord, this people, this whole place!' Another cry came, 'Holy Father, keep through thine own name those who thou hast given me!'[88]

On the morning of 25 March, he 'lifted up his hands as if in the attitude of pronouncing a blessing, and then sank down. Not a groan or a sigh, but only a quiver of the lip, and his soul was at rest.'[89]

## In Memory

The news of M'Cheyne's passing caused the city to bow a collective head in mourning. Andrew Bonar heard of the death as he was preparing his sermon for the Lord's Day. He raced down to Dundee and came upon a church in mourning. Hundreds of congregants filled the lower gallery. Weeping and crying could be heard out in the street. 'Such a scene of sorrow has not often been witnessed in Scotland,' he reported.[90]

Local newspapers memorialized M'Cheyne, with *The Courier* conceding: 'Although Mr McCheyne in his views of Church government, differed from ourselves, we have always thought that he was guided by principle and sincerity.' *The Witness* devoted numerous columns to M'Cheyne in three different editions. 'His precious life was short,' one column recalled, 'but he was an aged saint in Christian experience … into those few years there was compressed a life-time of ministerial usefulness.'[91]

The pastors within the M'Cheyne circle believed a heavy providence had struck. 'I dare not trust myself to speak of what I feel,' Robert Candlish wrote. 'How I admired and loved our departed friend.' Alexander Somerville longed that 'the death of Robert may be sanctified to me …. His death I do not think could ever have made a deeper impression; indeed, as the Lord honored him much in preaching and in his walk while alive, so he seems to have peculiar honor upon him in making his death so remarkable.'[92]

---

88. Ibid., p. 164.
89. Ibid., p. 165.
90. Ibid., p. 165.
91. Quoted in Yeaworth, p. 349.
92. Ibid., p. 350.

Some six to seven thousand people gathered for his funeral, proof of his remarkable life. St. Peter's erected a large tombstone in the church cemetery. The monument's inscription tried to capture M'Cheyne's faithfulness with a few lines:

> Walking closely with God, an example
> Of the Believers,
> In Word, in Conversation, in charity
> In spirit, in faith, in purity
> He ceased not, day and night, to labour
> and watch for souls;
> And was honoured by his Lord
> To draw many wanderers out of darkness
> Into the path of life.

## A Man of God

Robert Murray M'Cheyne's life was like a comet that streaks across the sky. It came almost as quickly as it went; but it was brilliant and captivating. He was familiar with the King's face and testified of the Lord's beauty. His all-encompassing devotion to Jesus Christ stood out to his contemporaries, and still rises in renown today. Love for Christ was the animating power that filled his moments. Whether in private or in public, he meant to seek Christ or serve Christ.

M'Cheyne once wrote to an inquirer: 'I do trust you are seeking hard after him whom your soul loveth. ... He is a powerful and precious Saviour, and happy are they who put their trust in him. He is the Rose of Sharon, lovely to look upon, having all divine and human excellencies meeting in himself.'[93] What remains for us to uncover is why and how his ardent Christ-centered devotion overflowed into every area of his life.

---

93. Bonar, *MAR*, p. 282.

CHAPTER 2

# M'Cheyne's Context and Influences

ROBERT Murray M'Cheyne was a capable theologian. He was more precise and aware than many people realize. However, before we notice his doctrinal convictions, we must notice the influences on M'Cheyene's theology. It did not arise *de novo* from his own intellect. Instead, he thrived in ministerial and confessional soil long tended by theological giants in the Scottish tradition.

Theological influences were not the only factors that formed M'Cheyne's heart for Christ. Contextual issues played a shaping role as well. Virtually every year of his short ministry saw momentous events mark the calendar. His entire ministry took place 'against a backdrop of astonishing change, profound and many-faceted, which left few areas of Scottish life untouched.'[1] One primary place of change lay in the Church of Scotland.

## M'Cheyne's Context: Evangelicalism Rising

In 1834, something momentous happened in the Kirk: evangelicals assumed 'a majority in the General Assembly for the first time in approximately one hundred years'.[2] The moderates, as they were popularly known, dominated the prior century of the church's

---

1. A. C. Cheyne, *Studies in Scottish Church History*, p. 107.
2. Ian Hamilton, 'Disruption,' in *Dictionary of Scottish Church History and Theology*, ed. Nigel M. de S. Cameron et al., p. 246.

political life. Moderatism is difficult to define. The term is somewhat similar to the moniker of 'Puritanism.' Both identifiers were employed pejoratively and lacked precise, universally agreed-upon characteristics.

Nonetheless, some broad features distinguished moderates in Scotland. First, the moderate party called for submission to authority, be it secular or spiritual. They also valued education and their intellectual worldview flourished under Enlightenment rationalism. Moderates prized a range of scholarly pursuits – literature, philosophy, history, and science – more than theological precision. Their love of liberal scholarship coincided with an aversion to confessional theology and subscription. Moderate preaching was not a biblical and theological encounter with Jesus Christ as much as it was a moralistic appeal. 'Elevating conduct over creed, they favored a new type of preaching that eschewed the traditionalists' weekly survey of "the scheme of salvation" and exchange moral discourses, stylishly expressed, for eloquent proclamation of the mysterious and the supernatural.'[3]

Hugh Miller, editor of the evangelical paper *The Witness*, liked to say that moderates were problematic and easy to spot. Edwin Sydney offered an overblown, yet typical description of moderates according to evangelicals:

A moderate divine is one who has a very moderate share of zeal for God. Consequently, a moderate divine contents himself with a moderate degree of labour in his Master's vineyard. A moderate divine is too polite and rational to give any credit to the antiquated divinity of our articles, homilies and liturgy. And, therefore, he seldom quotes them except it be to show his contempt for them, or to torture their meaning; nevertheless, a moderate divine is ready enough to subscribe to them, if by so doing he can get an immoderate share of church preferment. A moderate divine is always very cool and calm in his pulpit; he never argues, except when he is preaching, against such fathers of Israel as the pious and lowly Mr. Hallward; and then a moderate divine loses all his moderation. And so, I daresay, do the moderates of the kirk of Scotland, when denouncing the principles and

---

3. A. C. Cheyne, 'Moderates,' in *Encyclopedia of the Reformed Faith*, ed. Donald K. McKim, David F. Wright, p. 245.

conduct of the evangelical and zealous servants of Christ, who seek to do away with abuses which are favourable to moderatism. A moderate divine is usually an advocate for card-parties, and for all assemblies except religious ones; but thinks no name too hard for those who assemble to spend an hour or two in prayer, and hearing God's word.[4]

Evangelicals were not completely opposite from the moderates on every point. They were, however, at odds on the essential matters. Evangelicals emphasized the bold preaching of Jesus Christ, missionary and Bible societies, and a blossoming prayer movement in the Church. They taught that only Jesus Christ, not the state, has authority over the Church.

To many in the culture, evangelical piety appeared fresh and vibrant. Their convictions burned with a light and heat that had seemed to flicker and fade under moderate rule.

## The Ten Years' Conflict

M'Cheyne was licensed to the gospel ministry in 1835. His ministry thus took place 'within the controversial and prosperous period of the history of the Church of Scotland known as the "Ten Years' Conflict" which culminated in the Disruption of 1843.'[5] The Ten Years' Conflict was a battle for supremacy in the Church between the evangelicals and moderates. The key issue was the matter of patronage: who has the right to appoint ministers in the churches?

Moderates believed that the local church's patron possessed the right to call a minister. Such practice had a long history in Scotland. The common thinking was that because patrons supplied church buildings and ministerial salaries, they had the right to appoint ministers. Predictably, evangelicals stood against patronage. They declared Christ's headship over the church. Such headship demanded that the congregation, not the patron, call the minister.

The controversy raged throughout the 1830s and early 1840s. Power shifted back and forth between the parties, as legal battles ensued, capturing the nation's attention. The final break came just two months after M'Cheyne's death, when on 18 May 1843, the Disruption happened

---

4. Quoted in Buchanan, 1:176-77.
5. Yeaworth, p. 336.

– what one scholar calls, 'the most important event in the whole of Scotland's nineteenth-century history.'[6] Some four hundred and fifty ministers, along with at least half of the members, left the Church of Scotland to form the Free Church of Scotland. Evangelical doctrines and sympathies characterized early Free Church life.

M'Cheyne served as a leading light among the evangelicals during the Ten Years' Conflict. One historian named him the 'characteristic Evangelical of the period. ... The sacrifices and venturesomeness of the Disruption would have been impossible save in an atmosphere such as he created.'[7]

The Conflict created an environment in which M'Cheyne's stated views on Christ and the Church found a ready audience. He was a recognized leader among young evangelicals, often asked to stir up support for the cause throughout Britain, believing it to be 'a righteous struggle.'[8] He wrote letters, made speeches, organized meetings, and collected finances. He published articles arguing that Christ's headship is as significant as Christ's divinity.

In November of 1842, four hundred and sixty-five evangelical ministers gathered for a convocation in Edinburgh. They met to discuss the Church's present problems and possible solutions. M'Cheyne was present and took careful notes of the proceedings. He rose at one point to offer a proposal for 'united prayer which was widely circulated throughout the country.' He also led the meeting in prayer 'after a particularly tense and crucial debate.'[9] Chalmers' biographer recalled that 'the spirit of prayer ... from the lips of Mr M'Cheyne ... conveyed a profounder sense of the divine presence than we ever felt before or since in the most hallowed of our Christian assemblies.'[10]

The timing of M'Cheyne's rise should not be overlooked. The Ten Year's Conflict molded an ecclesiastical environment in which he could shine. In every way, from doctrinal matters to revival impulses, it was an ecclesiastical era suited perfectly for his personality and gifts.

---

6. Fry, p. 52.

7. Quoted in Yeaworth, p. 357.

8. M'Cheyne, *The Passionate Preacher,* p. 259.

9. Yeaworth, p. 342. For M'Cheyne's personal notes on the Convocation, see MACCH 1.16.

10. Quoted in Yeaworth, p. 342.

## Cultural and Philosophical Factors

Not only did the ecclesiastical context further M'Cheyne's status and ministry, the cultural context did as well. He lived in a philosophical milieu profoundly influenced by what was later termed 'The Enlightenment,' which thrived in Scotland more than in any other nineteenth-century country.[11]

The Scottish Enlightenment shaped an intellectual environment of rationality. Of particular importance, in M'Cheyne's context, was the realism that belonged to the Scottish common-sense philosophy. Thomas Reid, who first taught common sense philosophy, rejected the skepticism of David Hume. Reid's realistic philosophy explained how fundamental matters of reality are self-evident – we know them directly and intuitively. Because God was said to be the source of common-sense principles, Scottish Realism often cohered quickly with Christian belief. Ministers and leading lights such as Thomas Chalmers in Scotland and John Witherspoon in America passed this realism to the next generation of pastors and parishioners. The ordinary citizen of M'Cheyne's time wanted sensible – easily understood – arguments about eternity and piety. His plain preaching stood ready to meet the demand.

The intellectual worldview was not the only cultural current to amplify M'Cheyne's ministry. Another key was a cultural interest in homiletics and oratory. Biblical preaching was a valued cultural commodity in his time, one shaped by Romantic values and burgeoning Victorian ideals. In the Victorian era 'there was enormous interest in heroic preachers. That was one of the contributions of romanticism. The virtuosity of individual preachers was cherished, as were the talents of extraordinary singers or instrumentalists. In this respect preaching was a popular art.'[12] In a peculiar way, Lord's Day sermons were valued entertainment. Unconverted hearers flocked to the buildings of celebrated preachers, eager to hear a capable performance. M'Cheyne acknowledged and lamented his culture's enthrallment with preaching. He told St. Peter's: 'This is an age for hearing sermons; but there is little hearing the Word for all that.'[13]

---

11. David Bebbington, 'Enlightenment,' in *Dictionary of Scottish Church History and Theology*, p. 294.

12. Old, 6:348.

13. M'Cheyne, *TPH*, p. 89.

Just as the ecclesiastical scene set a stage for M'Cheyne, so did Scottish culture in the 1830s. Romantic emotion and soon-to-be-recognized Victorian values thrived. The appeal of his ministry was thus virtually guaranteed from the start. His spirituality wedded deep devotion and emotion to evangelical doctrine. His preaching was artistic, yet rational. For these reasons, one scholar rightly recognizes M'Cheyne 'as the patron saint of Victorian evangelicals.'[14]

## M'Cheyne's Theological and Ministerial Influences

No pastor comes to know Jesus Christ in a vacuum. Under God, movements and mentors mold men for the gospel ministry. This happened with M'Cheyne. He learned God's truth on the ancient paths and in the existing halls. Of all the people in his network, four men had a special influence on his life, theology, and ministry.

### Henry Duncan (1774–1846)

M'Cheyne and his siblings often holidayed with a maternal aunt in Ruthwell. On his many visits, M'Cheyne spent time with the local minister Henry Duncan – whom M'Cheyne called 'Uncle Henry.' Duncan was an immensely gifted pastor. He loved nature, was proficient in geography, and an ardent student of literature. He drafted laws for assisting the poor and increased educational standards. Duncan showed Robert how to marry artistic ability with a passion to bring souls to Christ. It was also at Ruthwell that M'Cheyne first saw what vibrant and intentional ministry to children could accomplish, as Duncan had an earnest outreach to children.

### Thomas Chalmers (1780–1847)

It is hard – maybe even impossible – to overstate Chalmers' influence on M'Cheyne. The venerable leader stamped his seal on every facet of Robert's thought and life. His class notes show how Chalmers' theological and ecclesiastical vision captivated him. Notes on Chalmers' class outlines abound.[15] Chalmers focused his doctrinal system on Jesus

---

14. Gribben, p. 191.
15. For example, see MACCH 1.7.

Christ, and so fueled M'Cheyne's fervor for the Savior. 'In Chalmers, more than any other person,' one scholar tells, 'McCheyne found the mould for his ecclesiastical and religious thought, and a worthy pattern for his own ministerial life.'[16]

## John Bonar (1801–1861)

Although M'Cheyne assisted John Bonar at Larbert and Dunipace for only ten months, the short season left a long impression. He referred genially to Bonar as 'my good bishop.'[17] Bonar's best quality was industry. He was responsible for more than seven hundred families and labored zealously to shepherd each one. His shepherding practice focused on home visitation. Under Bonar, M'Cheyne not only learned the value of diligent visitation, he learned its delight, admitting that visitation was his favorite part of ministry in his first charge. He also observed yet another successful scheme of ministering to children. 'I heard Mr Bonar teach his children ... in his inimitable way. He possesses a wonderful power of interesting children,' he wrote to his mother.[18]

In a roundabout way, Bonar influenced M'Cheyne's preaching – specifically the value of concise sermons. M'Cheyne remarked that while Bonar preached 'with great effect and plain common-sense power,' his sermons (which often exceeded ninety minutes) were too long. M'Cheyne reacted by preaching sermons of less than thirty-five minutes, a length that brought 'universal satisfaction.'[19]

## Robert Smith Candlish (1806–1873)

Candlish is probably the most underappreciated influence on M'Cheyne. Seven years older than M'Cheyne, Candlish 'was a wonderfully electric

---

16. Yeaworth, p. 79.
17. MACCH 2.6.16.
18. Ibid. 2.6.20.
19. Quoted in Yeaworth, p. 87. M'Cheyne's reaction was likely a youthful overreaction, for his sermons lengthened once installed at Dundee. Adam M'Cheyne remarks about his son's early sermons at St. Peter's: 'He was not easily satisfied with what he had done. As a consequence, he was apt to prolong his pulpit services to too great a length. Hence many who had no great concern about spiritual things became disgusted with his long sermons' (MACCH 2.7.50). Andrew Bonar concurs, saying it was not uncommon for M'Cheyne to be 'too long in his addresses' (MAR, p. 66).

preacher of the Evangel; and in his public prayers, as he led the devotions of his people, he was described ... as praying like an inspired Hebrew prophet.'[20] After the Disruption of 1843, Candlish was 'second only to Thomas Chalmers in his prestige in the new [Free Church], and he was its most prominent figure between Chalmers' death in 1847 and his own a quarter of a century later, being Moderator in 1861.'[21]

Candlish's influence on M'Cheyne lay primarily in the politics of ecclesiastical life. He appears to have seen M'Cheyne as an ideal model of evangelical Presbyterian ministry, writing: 'Assuredly he had more of the mind of his Master than almost any one I ever knew – and realized to me more of the likeness of the beloved disciple.'[22]

Candlish served as something like a denominational patron of M'Cheyne, assisting him in his passage through ordination. He lobbied for M'Cheyne's appointment to St. Peter's. He paved the way for M'Cheyne's role on the Mission of Inquiry to Palestine. He 'also showed a great interest in the 1839 awakening and McCheyne's part in it, and through him McCheyne was appointed to serve on various deputations and missions.'[23] At Candlish's behest, M'Cheyne contributed articles to the *Scottish Christian Herald*, and published chapters in *Family Worship* and *The Christian's Daily Companion*. Candlish also sent M'Cheyne 'to represent and explain the Church's position (on patronage) both in and out of Scotland.'[24]

## Historical Influences

M'Cheyne loved history. As with many in his circle, he drank deeply from the doctrinal wells of former theological giants. A careful study of his sermons, letters, and diary reveal three main historical influences.

### The Reformers

Reformation giants such as Martin Luther, John Calvin, and John Knox seasoned M'Cheyne's ministry. Direct quotes from the Reformers are not

---

20. Macleod, p. 271.
21. J. R. Wolffe, 'Candlish, Robert Smith,' in *Dictionary of Scottish Church History and Theology*, p. 134.
22. Quoted in Yeaworth, p. 141.
23. Yeaworth, p. 90.
24. Ibid., pp. 341; 344.

extensive, but they nonetheless cast a long shadow over his theological and spiritual program. M'Cheyne's hymn, 'Jehovah Tsidkenu,' has 'the watchword of the Reformers' as its superscription. From Martin Luther, he learned how to preach Christ. He adopted Luther's vision of preaching as his own: 'The gospel is the true alluring speech that draws the heart of man.'[25] He also channeled Luther in speaking against 'the splendid sins of humanity,' urging hearers to cling to Christ alone for salvation.[26] He also considered Luther a model of diligent and fervent prayer.[27]

After returning from the Mission of Inquiry, M'Cheyne's labor found him increasingly involved with Christians of all denominations. Ecumenical action brought him criticism. 'Indeed, he so much longed for a scriptural unity,' Bonar remarks, 'that some time after, when the General Assembly had repealed the statute of 1799, he embraced the opportunity of showing his desire for unity, by inviting two dissenting brethren to his pulpit, and then writing in defense of his conduct when attacked.'[28] One such writing was a letter to the editor of the *Dundee Warder*, dated 6 July 1842. In the letter, M'Cheyne called on John Calvin as a witness to prove that his ecumenical practice was thoroughly in step with Reformation principles.[29] Where John Calvin's teaching on the church gave a doctrinal spine to M'Cheyne's efforts for ecumenicity, John Knox's spirit gave him a ministerial fire.[30] The Scottish Reformer exuded courage in truth, and convinced M'Cheyne that the gospel could conquer a country for Christ.

## The Puritans

M'Cheyne immersed himself in the Puritan fathers and their theological children, freely referencing figures such as Thomas Boston, John Flavel, John Owen, and John Bunyan. Richard Baxter was especially prominent for M'Cheyne. After reading Baxter's *Call to the Unconverted*, M'Cheyne wrote:

---

25. M'Cheyne, *TPP*, p. 75.
26. Ibid., *TPH*, p. 33.
27. Bonar, *MAR*, pp. 255, 366; M'Cheyne, *BOF*, p. 49.
28. Ibid., p. 139.
29. Ibid., pp. 560, 562.
30. M'Cheyne, *OTS*, p. 168; Bonar, *MAR*, p. 196.

> Though Baxter's lips have long in silence hung,
> And death long hush'd that sinner-wakening tongue;
> Yet still, though dead, he speaks aloud to us all;
> And from the grave still issues forth his 'Call.'[31]

Baxter's evangelistic zeal captured M'Cheyne and caused him to declare in an ordination sermon: 'O for a pastor who unites the deep knowledge of Edwards, the vast statements of Owen, and the vehement appeals of Richard Baxter!'[32]

Another Puritan who influenced M'Cheyne was Samuel Rutherford. He loved to feast on Rutherford's 'flame of grace.'[33] In one sermon, he admitted, 'How humbling it is to read Rutherford.'[34] A friend recalled that Rutherford's *Letters* were M'Cheyne's 'daily delight,' and that 'like Rutherford his adoring contemplations naturally gathered round them the imagery and language of the Song of Solomon.'[35] Rutherford's insistence on Christ's sweetness and loveliness shaped M'Cheyne's romantic Christology. He found in Rutherford a soul-mate in Christ-centered spirituality.

## Jonathan Edwards and David Brainerd

M'Cheyne interacts with Edwards and Brainerd far more than any other authors. The influence of Edwards and Brainerd are taken together because they represent a united model of piety and ministry. Edwards' best-selling book was his edited volume, *Life of David Brainerd*. Brainerd represented Edwards' ideal for spirituality, one of asceticism, self-examination, and Christological focus.

On 20 March 1832, M'Cheyne wrote in his diary: 'Read part of the life of Jonathan Edwards. How feeble does my spark of Christianity appear beside such a sun! But even his was a borrowed light, and the same source is still open to enlighten me.'[36] This first-recorded encounter with the Northampton pastor was powerful enough to

---

31. Bonar, *MAR*, p. 25.
32. Ibid., p. 363.
33. Ibid., p. 184.
34. MACCH 1.10.
35. Hamilton, p. 222. See also, MAR, p. 145.
36. Bonar, *MAR*, p. 14. See also Loane, p. 146.

cause M'Cheyne to purchase Edwards' works three months later.[37] 'It was [during his first pastoral charge] ... that [M'Cheyne] began to study so closely the works of Jonathan Edwards – reckoning them a mine to be wrought, and if wrought, sure to repay the toil,' Bonar explains.[38] M'Cheyne's writings uncover a longing that his 'heart and understanding may grow together' like Edwards.[39] He found 'help and freedom' from Edwards' instruction on prayer.[40] He encouraged William Chalmers Burns to remember Edwards' 'magnificent' resolutions.[41] He urges Christians to imitate Edwards' example.[42] Near the end of his ministry M'Cheyne called Edwards 'one of the holiest and most eminent divines that ever lived.'[43]

Edwards gave M'Cheyne a theological vision for revival and convinced him of how to preach God's sovereign grace in a way that infuses the affections with sweetness and love. Brainerd showed M'Cheyne what it means to center evangelism on Christ's loveliness. He told St. Peter's that 'David Brainerd's people were most deeply affected because Christ was so lovely.'[44] In another sermon, he said: 'I remember David Brainerd used to say that he loved to see souls saved, not so much for the sake of the souls that were saved, as for the joy and glory it gave to the Lord Jesus.'[45]

## Conclusion

M'Cheyne's ministry happened at a time when coalescing movements in Scotland prepared a platform for him to shine. In almost every way, he embodied the distinguishing features of the revived evangelical theology and piety of the 1830s. The cresting evangelical tide in Scotland carried him to prominence that was atypical for a pastor so young.

Forces beyond the ecclesiastical realm further provided a stage for M'Cheyne. Common sense philosophy and romanticism created

---

37. Bonar, *MAR*, p. 15.
38. Ibid., p. 33.
39. Ibid., p. 16.
40. Ibid., p. 56.
41. Ibid., p. 242.
42. Ibid., pp. 363, 377. See also, M'Cheyne, *TPP*, p. 306.
43. M'Cheyne, *HTD*, p. 16.
44. Ibid., *OTS*, p. 52.
45. Ibid., *TPP*, p. 166.

an intellectual and emotional environment suited – and eager – for a ministry like M'Cheyne's. Influences such as Chalmers and Candlish ensured that he ascended to a position of prominence. The Reformers, the Puritans, Edwards, and Brainerd imparted and confirmed a passionate Christological spirituality.

The theology behind such spirituality now demands our attention.

# PART 2:
# Foundations for Holiness

CHAPTER 3

# M'Cheyne and Knowing Christ

ONE forgotten theological titan of the nineteenth-century Scottish church is John Duncan – affectionately called 'Rabbi' Duncan. Born in 1796, Duncan struggled to find rest in orthodox Christianity, even while he was at divinity halls of the Associate Presbytery (at Whitburn) and then the Church of Scotland (at Aberdeen). He variously embraced pantheism and Sabellianism. In 1826, he was converted to Christ and eventually became a missionary to Jews in Budapest, Hungary. At the Disruption in 1843, Duncan joined the Free Church and was elected Professor of Hebrew at New College, Edinburgh.

A historian describes Duncan as 'at once the most profound and versatile of scholars, one of the humblest believers, and one of the most erratic and absentminded of men.'[1] *The Expository Times* reminisced of Duncan by calling him

> the singular character about whom so many hypothetical stories are told, it is not too much to say that he was one of the richest minds of our time; a man with visions of genius, though also with erratic ways; a man of extraordinary learning, but without the aptitude for systematic, circumstantial teaching; a thinker teeming with ideas of original order and lofty scope; the simplest, devoutest, most reverent, most unworldly of natures; a man at his best in occasional utterances and flashes of luminous converse.[2]

---

1. Macleod, pp. 282-83.
2. Hastings, p. 442.

Some of Duncan's more famous aphorisms encourage the soul. When administering the Lord's Supper, especially in later life, Duncan was often seen at the Table with tears pouring down his face. He considered forgiveness through Christ's blood an overwhelmingly joyous thought. One time, when passing out the elements, Duncan noticed a woman crying and trembling to take the cup. She did not know if she was worthy enough to commune with Christ. Duncan leaned over to her and whispered in her ear, 'It's for a sinner.'[3] Or, there was the time when he held his nine-month-old grandson and declared, 'You are a little sinner.' A family member immediately objected to such a frank admission of depravity, 'But he is not responsible!' Duncan replied, 'He is responsible, but I pray he has a Sponsor.'[4]

Duncan was never shy of throwing a punch in his assessment of preachers, theologians, or famous figures. He remarked of the Rev. F. W. Robertson: 'Robertson believed that Christ did something or other, which, somehow or other, had some connexion or other with salvation.' Of Archbishop Whately, Duncan remembered: 'I once heard Archbishop Whately, to my great disappointment. He was very dull and wish-washy. He preached on good behavior, but it was blanched morality.' Duncan commented memorably on Wesley's hymns: 'I have a great liking for many of Wesley's Hymns; but when I read some of them, I ask, "What's become of your Free-will now, friend?"'[5]

Rabbi Duncan was one of M'Cheyne's ministerial friends. They were often found assisting Alexander Moody-Stuart during communion seasons in Edinburgh. Although they loved each other in the Lord, they possessed noticeable disagreements and differences. Moody-Stuart spoke of 'a general unlikeness' between them.

Duncan's famous satirical ability was known to focus on M'Cheyne at times. In the M'Cheyne circle, friends never forgot one time when Duncan's pith packed an unusual punch. 'M'Cheyne's mind,' Duncan carped, 'plays about the lighter aspects of theology.'[6] Modern assessments of M'Cheyne's doctrinal ability agree with Duncan's

---

3. Moody-Stuart, p. 100.
4. Ibid., p. 201.
5. David Brown, p. 401.
6. Moody-Stuart, p. 47.

criticism.[7] He was an effective preacher, the trope goes, but not precise – maybe not even very proficient – in theology and doctrine. The original context of Duncan's quote appears to drive at M'Cheyne's supposed inability to be severe in his doctrine.

We need to reassess Duncan's verbal volley. M'Cheyne's lack of doctrinal creativity does not reveal disinterest or carelessness in theology. Sure, his theology should never be called 'original' or 'innovative.' He subscribed happily to the Westminster Confession of Faith, proclaiming its substance as nothing less than the summary of biblical doctrine. Charles Hodges' quip that no new theology ever originated at Princeton Seminary would have resonated with M'Cheyne.

M'Cheyne believed theology was useful and beneficial. A proper reckoning with his doctrinal sensibility realizes that he was an eminent *practical theologian*. No part of that two-word label should be underplayed. All his practice was theological, and all his theology was practical. A contemporary of M'Cheyne decided, 'With all his poetry [M'Cheyne] did not care for what was speculative, but liked all that was practical; practical in theology, practical in spiritual exercise, practical in dealing with the conscience, practical in duty.'[8] The conclusion was not meant as a slight against M'Cheyne. His emphasis on doctrine *for life* unveils how far he plumbed divine truth. Only those who have truly understood the deep things of God can make them clear and useful for Christians. Foggy views of doctrine create a muddled spirituality. But, as his ministry shows, clarity of truth leads to luminous piety.

## M'Cheyne's Theology: Covenant and Calvinism

M'Cheyne's theology and spirituality were in harmony with the Westminster Standards: the Confession of Faith together with the Larger and Shorter Catechisms. Because he very rarely quoted from the Standards in his sermons, some have stated, 'If by some strange

---

7. For example, David Yeaworth concludes, 'While there is a strong undercurrent of doctrine in McCheyne's preaching, and although he kept abreast of contemporary thought as it was related to Evangelicalism, he did not consider it to be expedient to give a prominent place to theology as such, except as it touched upon his chief object of evangelism and Christian nurture' (Yeaworth, p. 228).

8. Moody-Stuart, p. 49.

chance all the copies of the Westminster Confession had disappeared it would be totally impossible to reconstruct the barest outline of it' from M'Cheyne's ministry.[9]

However, any sane conclusion of M'Cheyne's teaching demonstrates how he was a Westminster man at his core. He subscribed to the Standards at his ordination and his commitment never wavered. Piercing the perception of M'Cheyne as a less than capable Reformed theologian is actually quite simple. We can begin by noticing his emphasis on the centrality of covenant theology.

## A Covenant Theologian

Previous studies of M'Cheyne's theology fail to see the consistency and depth of his reflections on God's covenants. The oversight is likely due to M'Cheyne having never lectured on covenant theology at length. Yet, a study of his writings exposes how the covenant occupies a primary place in his thinking.

A covenantal reading of redemptive history is a hallmark of the Westminster Confession. B. B. Warfield famously – and loquaciously – declared: 'The architectonic principle of the Westminster Confession is supplied by the schematization of the Federal theology, which had obtained by this time in Britain, as on the Continent, a dominant position as the most commodious mode of presenting the *corpus* of Reformed doctrine.'[10] Warfield's language is almost too wordy to

9. Andrew L. Drummond and James Bulloch, *The Church in Victorian Scotland, 1843–1874* (Edinburgh: Saint Andrews Press, 1975), p. 301. Such rare mentions include a quotation of Shorter Catechism 37 in Robert Murray M'Cheyne, *New Testament Sermons* (Edinburgh: Banner of Truth, 2004), p. 186; a quotation of Shorter Catechism 1 in Robert Murray M'Cheyne, *A Basket of Fragments* (1848; repr., Inverness, Scotland: Christian Focus, 1975), p. 167; and specific interaction with Westminster Confession of Faith 25.1 in M'Cheyne, *BOF*, p. 124. He also alluded to the Shorter Catechism by way of warning individuals not to rely on religious knowledge. M'Cheyne, *BOF*, p. 98; Robert Murray M'Cheyne, *The Passionate Preacher: Sermons of Robert Murray McCheyne* (Fearn, Scotland: Christian Focus, 1999), pp. 32, 38, 39, 81; *Robert Murray M'Cheyne, The Believer's Joy* (1858; repr., Glasgow: Free Presbyterian Publications, 1987), pp. 14, 44.

10. B. B. Warfield, 'The Westminster Assembly and Its Work,' in *The Works of Benjamin B. Warfield*, ed. E. D. Warfield et al., 10 vols. (1931; repr., Grand Rapids: Baker, 1981), 6:56 (emphasis original).

understand today. What the Lion of Princeton says is this: covenant theology provides the structure to Reformed doctrine.

M'Cheyne's sermon on Hebrews 8:6 is the best starting point into his covenantal doctrine. The message is classic covenantal theology in miniature. He begins by '[inquiring] into the covenants that are spoken of in the Word of God.'[11] He explains the standard Reformed perspective on the Covenant of Works, the covenants with Noah, Abraham, Moses, and the New Covenant secured in Christ.[12] For M'Cheyne, covenant theology is not a speculative approach to redemptive history, but proof of 'the *amazing love of God* ... [for] the covenant which he made with Noah was a covenant of grace; and the covenant he made at Sinai, was also a covenant of grace; and the covenant that was made with Christ was a covenant of grace.'[13] Noticeably absent from this sermon are the Davidic Covenant and the Covenant of Redemption.

Although M'Cheyne gives scant attention to God's covenant with David, he consistently extols the *pactum salutis*. In fact, the Covenant of Redemption – the intra-Trinitarian covenant in eternity – saturates his preaching.[14] He delights in how this covenant displays Christ's eternal love, declaring, 'The Bible assures us that this feeling of compassion for sinners that care not for Him existed in the bosom of Christ before the world was. It was this feeling that moved Him to enter into covenant with His Father in the eternity that is past, that He would undertake the doing and suffering of all that was needful in the stead of guilty sinners.'[15]

M'Cheyne was careful not to detach covenant theology from Jesus Christ. He fixed God's covenant promises to Jesus Christ. When speaking about the Mosaic Covenant, he preaches: 'I believe that we do not rightly understand the old covenant unless we understand it thus,

---

11. M'Cheyne, *SOH*, p. 109.
12. Ibid., *SOH*, pp. 109-12. For M'Cheyne's comments on the Shorter Catechism's teaching on the Covenant of Works and Covenant of Grace, see MACCH 1.7.
13. M'Cheyne, *SOH*, p. 112 (emphasis original).
14. Robert Murray M'Cheyne, *Old Testament Sermons* (Edinburgh: Banner of Truth, 2004), p. 87; Robert Murray M'Cheyne, *From the Preacher's Heart* (1846; repr., Fearn, Scotland: Christian Focus, 1993), p. 400; M'Cheyne, *NTS*, p. 13; Bonar, *MAR*, p. 375; M'Cheyne, *TPP*, p. 15; M'Cheyne, *SOH*, pp. 118, 121-22.
15. M'Cheyne, *SOH*, p. 188. See also, M'Cheyne, *OTS*, p. 87; M'Cheyne, *TPH*, p. 400.

unless we see it as making them long for the coming of Christ.'[16] When defining the Covenant of Grace, he says: 'God makes the covenant with a sinner when he brings the sinner to lay hold on Christ; then the covenant made with Christ is put into the sinner's hand, its conditions being all fulfilled already by Jesus.'[17] He understands the New Covenant as 'the gospel covenant'[18] that joins us to Christ,[19] who is its surety and mediator.[20]

Centering the covenant on Christ is appropriate because Christ is a 'covenant Saviour,'[21] 'covenant head,'[22] and the 'Angel of the Covenant.'[23] Through Christ's saving work we are 'brought into the bonds of the covenant,'[24] and thus become Christ's covenant people.[25] M'Cheyne's covenant Christology reaches its climax when he says that not only has God made 'but one covenant – that is, with Christ and all in him,'[26] but also Christ Himself is the covenant.[27]

M'Cheyne's covenant theology illustrates how he tended to engage in his practical theology. The covenant frames his common encouragements to Christ-centered piety. Perfect happiness and holiness 'is all in the covenant.'[28] Additionally, the covenant imparts confidence for the increase of grace, because through it we are united to Christ and thus 'there is covenant certainty about our holiness. It shall abide forever, for the Spirit shall abide with us forever.'[29]

The covenant undergirds M'Cheyne's spirituality of suffering. He exhorted believers to see affliction as a covenantal act to grow the

---

16. Ibid., *SOH*, p. 161. For further reflection on the Mosaic Covenant, see M'Cheyne, *TPP*, p. 55; M'Cheyne, *SOH*, pp. 122, 160-61, 184.
17. Ibid., *TPP*, p. 15.
18. Ibid., *TPP*, p. 50.
19. Ibid., *TBJ*, p. 99.
20. Ibid., *TPP*, p. 155.
21. Ibid., *TPH*, p. 70.
22. Ibid., *TPH*, p. 149.
23. Ibid., *TPP*, p. 87; Bonar, *MAR*, p. 307.
24. Ibid., *TPH*, p. 430.
25. Ibid., *TPP*, p. 58.
26. Ibid., *TPH*, p. 256.
27. Ibid., *TPH*, p. 73; M'Cheyne, *TPP*, p. 124; M'Cheyne, *NTS*, p. 23.
28. Ibid., *TPH*, p. 171.
29. Ibid., *TPP*, p. 212.

church's love.[30] Much of his thought stemmed from Ezekiel 20:37, where God warns, 'I will cause you to pass under the rod, and I will bring you into the bond of the covenant.' M'Cheyne meant for people to know how God uses hardship and pain not just to bring into, but also to keep His people in the covenant. After William Burns went through a season of sickness, M'Cheyne wrote a letter of encouragement. After quoting the verse from Ezekiel, M'Cheyne penned, 'Sweet rod that drives the soul into such a precious resting place.'[31]

Love for Christ is the spiritual apex point of covenant theology – as it is in every loci of theology. In his exposition of the various types found in the Tabernacle, M'Cheyne comes to the ornaments placed on the priest's shoulders. He asserted, 'These chains and sockets of gold are the love of Christ – his electing love – his drawing love – his covenant love.'[32]

## A Calvinist Theologian

Think of M'Cheyne's doctrinal program with the analogy of a house. Christ is the cornerstone; covenant theology is the foundation. The house has four main living areas: the doctrines of election, sin, salvation, and sanctification. That M'Cheyne lived in these areas is indisputable. Never does a sermon pass without him illuminating at least one of these truths.

## (1) God's Sovereignty

M'Cheyne's commitment to 'Calvinism' was predictable. His ministry began at a time when 'the Calvinism of the Westminster Standards was restored and adhered to by moderates and evangelicals alike, and was the popular religious thought of the day.'[33] Also, God's sovereign decree was the first subject he studied after his conversion.

Whereas many think God's election is a dry dogma, M'Cheyne considered it enlivening. 'God alone can bring you into the covenant,' he proclaimed. 'A Sovereign Almighty Jehovah must do it or it will be

---

30. Ibid., *BOF*, p. 39. See also, M'Cheyne, *OTS*, p. 137-38; M'Cheyne, *MAR*, pp. 241, 316.
31. Ibid., *MAR*, p. 241. The Scripture reference is Ezekiel 20:37.
32. Bonar, *MAR*, p. 485.
33. Yeaworth, pp. 226-27.

left undone.'[34] M'Cheyne sharpened convictions about God's decree while at the Divinity Hall. Copious notes accompany the decree in a notebook entry titled, 'The Leading Doctrines of Christianity.' No doctrine receives more attention in this notebook than the following truth: 'Salvation is only by the Free Grace of God in Christ Jesus Our Lord.'[35]

Most of M'Cheyne's congregation believed in God's sovereign decree. Therefore, it is rare to find his preaching include a precise defense of election. Instead, he asserted simply, 'Ah! my brethren, those who deny election, deny that God can have mercy. O it is a sweet truth that God can have mercy!'[36]

A glory of election is how it removes all human contribution to salvation. 'So long as a person has hope of saving himself, of reforming, praying, weeping out his sins, so long he keeps his religion up. But when he is brought to see that he can do nothing to save himself, that it signifies just nothing, his heart dies within him,' M'Cheyne explained.[37] But having one's heart die, does not mean the death of hope and joy. In fact, for M'Cheyne, God's sovereignty was a great reason to sing with cheer! His hymn, 'I Am Debtor,' sings forth:

> Chosen not for good in me;
> Wakened up from wrath to flee,
> Hidden in the Saviour's side,
> By the Spirit sanctified,
> Teach me, Lord, on earth, to show,
> By my love, how much I owe.[38]

## (2) Human Depravity

M'Cheyne believed any soul must discover the terror of sin if it is to see God's glory in Jesus Christ. No stench of hypocrisy excited his emphasis on sin. He focused on sin with his congregation because he had seen the depths of sin in his heart. The searching power of self-examination was

---

34. M'Cheyne, *TPP*, p. 16.
35. MACCH 1.5.
36. M'Cheyne, *BOF*, p. 47.
37. Ibid., *OTS*, p. 99.
38. Bonar, *MAR*, p. 588.

necessary if one was to love Christ truly. M'Cheyne urged a good friend in ministry, 'Pray for more knowledge of your own heart – of the total depravity of it – of the awful depths of corruption that are there.'[39] The Lord answered his personal prayers on the matter. He regularly probed his heart and discovered a darkness that caused him to feel 'broken under a sense of my exceeding wickedness.'[40] Two particular sins plagued him.

*The sin of pride.* M'Cheyne's war against self-exaltation was constant. The struggle came from external and internal forces. Unbroken ministerial success caused the former, while innate stirrings to vanity motivated the latter. After an unusually well-attended Lord's Day, M'Cheyne asked, 'Shall I call the liveliness of this day a gale of the Spirit, or was all natural? I know that all was not of grace; the self-admiration, the vanity, the desire of honour, the bitterness – these were all breaths of earth or hell.'[41] Following another Sunday in which his preaching was praised, he remarked, 'I fear some like the messenger, not the message; and I fear I am so vain as to love that love.'[42]

Sabbath ministry was the regular soil in which his pride festered. He wrote after a day of effective preaching: 'In both discourses I can look back on many hateful thoughts of pride, and self-admiration, and love of praise, stealing the heart out of the service.'[43] His self-interest bulged enough to require correction. He always considered his seasons of sickness as God's chastisement for pride. During one prolonged period of illness, he told his sister Eliza that God had sent the disease to 'teach me that He can save and feed the people without any help of mine.'[44]

While the rising of pride was constant, M'Cheyne considered another sin as his deepest fleshly longing. *The sin of lust.* He disclosed, 'The lust of praise has ever been my besetting sin.'[45] In his *Personal Reformation*, he admitted, 'I am tempted to think that I am now an established Christian – that I have overcome this or that lust so long ....

---

39. Ibid., p. 242.
40. Ibid., p. 56.
41. Ibid., p. 44.
42. Ibid., p. 44.
43. Ibid., p. 43. See also Bonar, *MAR*, p. 45.
44. M'Cheyne, *Familiar Letters*, pp. 134-35.
45. Bonar, *MAR*, p. 36.

This is a lie of Satan.' He goes on to write: 'I am helpless in respect of every lust that ever was, or ever will be, in the human heart.'[46] An 1842 letter to Robert Macdonald of Blairgowrie reveals the depth of M'Cheyne's struggle:

> I think I never was brought to feel the wickedness of my heart as I do now. Yet I do not feel it as many sweet Christians do, while they are high above it, and seem to look down into a depth of iniquity, deep, deep in their bosoms. Now, it appears to me as if my feet were actually in the miry clay, and I only wonder that I am kept from open sin. My only refuge is in the word, 'I will put my Spirit within you.' It is only by being made partakers of the *divine nature* that I can escape the corruption that is in the world through lust.[47]

M'Cheyne spoke of lust in two different ways. More often than not, he understood it in the broad sense of 'sinful passion' – a temptation directed to many different vices.[48] Yet, he almost spoke as often about lust as sinful sexual desire.[49] Nothing in his writings or sermons allows us to specify the exact nature of his struggle. It seems best to conclude that he waged a prolonged battle with those passions typical of an ambitious, young, and single man.

As mentioned above, he saw self-examination as a key duty in the Christian life. Without wise, biblical introspection, why would a believer increasingly lean on Jesus Christ? He knew that deeper discoveries of Christ's love stem from uncovering the depths of sin. 'The more you feel your weakness, the amazing depravity of your heart,' he counseled, 'the more need have you to lean on Jesus.'[50] A clear sense of sin is necessary

---

46. Ibid., pp. 153-54.
47. Ibid., p. 275 (emphasis original).
48. Ibid., pp. 351, 369, 387, 392, 400, 533; M'Cheyne, *HTD*, p. 63; M'Cheyne, *BOF*, pp. 39, 92, 100, 104, 140, 171, 185; M'Cheyne, *TPH*, pp. 39, 41, 42, 47, 101, 111, 115, 141, 146, 164, 168, 181, 210, 227, 230, 240, 241, 242, 260, 344, 367, 369, 375, 410, 421, 426, 450, 464, 474, 516; M'Cheyne, *SOH*, pp. 13, 24, 42, 107, 170; M'Cheyne, *NTS*, pp. 56, 58, 90, 121, 148, 229, 230, 318; *TPP*, pp. 64, 86, 87, 130, 164, 203, 223, 238, 243, 253, 282, 286, 331; M'Cheyne, *OTS*, p. 60.
49. Ibid., pp. 352, 437; M'Cheyne, *HTD*, p. 75; M'Cheyne, *SOH*, p. 23; M'Cheyne, *TPP*, pp. 13, 45, 132, 224, 307; M'Cheyne, *TBJ*, p. 96; M'Cheyne, *TPH*, pp. 74, 129, 250, 312, 421; M'Cheyne, *BOF*, p. 186; M'Cheyne, *NTS*, pp. 80, 180, 277-79, 282, 307, 310.
50. Ibid., pp. 526-27.

to any apprehension of Christ's grace. He proclaimed, 'Be determined to know the worst of yourself; for thus only will you see the desirableness of conversion – the excellency of Christ.'[51] He further told a young minister: 'I believe we cannot lay down the guilt of man – his total depravity, and the glorious gospel of Christ, too clearly; that we cannot urge men to embrace and flee too warmly.'[52]

The familiar landing point for his piety was love for Christ. What is perhaps more unfamiliar in his ministry is how such love drives people to Christ. Much of the Reformed tradition advocates a particular sequence in gospel preaching: declare the terrors of the law to drive a person from self and into Christ. M'Cheyne thought the preacher had a more magnetic power at his disposal than fear of the law. 'You *may* be moved with fear, as Noah was, but you *must* be drawn by love. I believe that never a soul was converted without a sight of the God of glory,' he preached.[53] He maintained that while the law's terror is a proper means to induce fear of judgment, it cannot cause a sinner to close with Christ. For that to happen, the sinner must look upon God's eternal love in Christ:

> It is commonly thought that preaching the holy law is the most awakening truth in the Bible, – that by it the mouth is stopped, and all the world becomes guilty before God; and, indeed, I believe this is the most ordinary mean which God makes use of. And yet to me there is something far more awakening in the sight of a Divine Saviour freely offering Himself to every one of the human race.[54]

## (3) The Son's Beauty

Nothing astonished M'Cheyne as Christ's desire to save sinners. The Savior's errand of salvation was entrancing, ravishing, and overwhelming. Thus, no sermon was ever complete without publishing Christ's love for sinners.

Some considered M'Cheyne's sweet enticements to close with Christ little more than youthful, evangelical zeal. Yet, he believed

---

51. M'Cheyne, *TPH*, p. 43.

52. Bonar, *MAR*, p. 363.

53. M'Cheyne, *BOF*, p. 81 (emphasis original).

54. Bonar, *MAR*, p. 326.

that preaching Christ in this way was required. He reminded a fellow minister to 'never forget that the end of a sermon is the salvation of the people.'[55] He confessed to St. Peter's: 'I have sought to preach to all, that the veil was rent and that every sinner might enter; that Christ was lifted up, and that every sinner might look to Him and live.'[56] Apparently, his indefatigable gospel preaching troubled many who sat in the pews. He told of those who were 'quite offended because we preach Christ to the vilest of sinners.'[57] But he was undeterred, proclaiming, 'This is the chief object of the Bible, to show you the work, the beauty, the glory, the excellency of this High Priest.'[58] He promised he would not stop proclaiming 'in accents of tenderness … the simple message of redeeming love – that the wrath of God is abiding on sinners, but that Christ is a Saviour freely offered to them, just as they are.'[59]

M'Cheyne aimed to preach Christ as beautiful and wonderful. Looking on Jesus is the most attractive and arresting sight known to man. He pitied churches whose minister spoke of Christ with detached or aloof tones. Once, Andrew Bonar preached at St. Peter's on Isaiah 33:17 and 'Thine eyes shall see the King in His beauty.' M'Cheyne critiqued his friend's sermon as not addressing the unbeliever with enough earnestness. 'You and I and many, I trust, in our congregations shall see the King in His beauty. But, my brother, you forgot there might be many listening to you to-night, who, unless they are changed by the grace of God, shall never see Him in His beauty.'[60]

M'Cheyne had a theological reason for concentrating on Christ's loveliness. He believed beholding such beauty is the ordinary way that the Spirit draws the sinner. In one letter, he wrote:

---

55. Ibid., p. 329.

56. M'Cheyne, *OTS*, p. 101.

57. Ibid., *TPH*, p. 381.

58. Ibid., *SOH*, p. 87.

59. Ibid., *TPH*, p. 318. His concentration on the gospel message goes all the way back to his days at the Divinity Hall. He recorded in a notebook: 'Subjects for the Pulpit.' One annotation reads, 'In demonstrating the guilt and the remedy—the danger of rejecting the duty of embracing the gospel—you are dealing with the great elements of preaching' (MACCH 1.7).

60. Marjory Bonar, *Reminiscences*, p. 132.

I do trust that you are seeking hard after Him whom your soul loveth. He is not far from any one of us. He is a powerful and precious Saviour, and happy are they who put their trust in Him. He is the Rose of Sharon, lovely to look upon, having all divine and human excellencies meeting in Himself; and yet he is the Lily of the Valleys, – meek and lowly in heart, willing to save the vilest. He answers the need of your soul. You are all guilt; He is a fountain to wash you. You are all naked; He has a wedding garment to cover you. You are dead; He is the life. You are all wounds and bruises; He is the Balm of Gilead. His righteousness is broader than your sin; and then He is so free.[61]

Knowing God's love in Christ is the magnetic center of M'Cheyne's theology. Because Christ is 'altogether lovely' and came to earth on an 'errand ... of purest love,' a true gospel ministry overflows with gospel ardour.[62] If a minister is to be found faithful and fruitful, he must forsake everything to follow Christ because he has 'seen the loveliness of Christ.'[63]

## (4) The Spirit's Efficacy

A rich Trinitarianism permeates M'Cheyne's doctrine. Just as he gloried in the Father's sovereignty and the Son's beauty, he relied on the Spirit's efficacy. His dependence on the Spirit was obvious from the start at St. Peter's. His first sermon as minister took Isaiah 61:1-3 as the text: 'The Spirit of the LORD God is upon me; because the LORD hath anointed me to preach good tidings.... (KJV).' Ministerial success needs fullness from the Spirit. Power in ministry does not come from increased talents, skills, or personality. What every preacher needs is the Spirit's filling. 'The more anointing of the Holy Spirit,' he reasoned, 'the more success will the minister have.'[64] Further, he extolled the Holy Spirit, calling Him the 'greatest of all the privileges of a Christian,'[65] adding, 'It is

---

61. Bonar, *MAR*, p. 322.
62. M'Cheyne, *TPH*, p. 180. M'Cheyne's teaching on Christ's loveliness and love for sinners is vast, saturating his entire sermon catalog. For representative sermons, see 'The Love of Christ' on 2 Corinthians 5:14 *TPH*, pp. 44-54, and 'Who Shall Separate Us from the Love of Christ?' on Romans 8:35-37 in *TPH*, pp. 341-48.
63. Ibid., *TBJ*, p. 84.
64. Bonar, *MAR*, p. 530.
65. M'Cheyne, *OTS*, p. 74.

sweet to get the love of Christ; but I will tell you what is equally as sweet – that is to receive the Spirit of Christ.'[66]

M'Cheyne located the Spirit's work in two vital areas of doctrine: regeneration and sanctification. He spoke of the Spirit as God's agent unto conversion, the divine, personal power that renovates the soul. The Spirit's work starts with conviction of sin. Then, the Spirit convinces the sinner of Christ's righteousness. As M'Cheyne instructed, the Spirit always makes us 'look to a pierced Christ.'[67] On the matter of sanctification, he stated: 'In the sanctification of the people of God, though means are used, yet the word is not by might, nor by power, but by God's Spirit.'[68] Always eager to emphasize the ordinary means of grace, he did not doubt *how* the Spirit grows God's people in Christ: 'It is in learning, in reading, in remembering, in meditating on the Word of God that the Spirit works in us to will and do of God's good pleasure.'[69]

God's truth is not merely to be known; it must be experienced. M'Cheyne understood the experiential joy of life in the Spirit. He reminded a friend:

> Learn to hold intimate communion with God. The Spirit of God will continually be lifting the heart to sweet adoring thoughts of God. Through Jesus we have access by one Spirit to the Father. The Spirit is one with the Father and the Son and wherever he dwells he will be lifting himself toward God. If you are the temple of the Holy Ghost, then what sweet fellowship you will have with the Father and the Son. Oh, what adoring looks at Jesus will not the Spirit make you cast.[70]

## Preacher of the Free Offer

M'Cheyne's emphases on covenant theology, God's sovereignty, human depravity, the Son's beauty, and the Spirit's efficacy are wed together in his free offer of the gospel. The best way to describe his identity as a gospel minister is that he was *a preacher of the free offer of Christ's love for sinners.*

---

66. Ibid., *BOF*, p. 42.
67. Ibid., *TPH*, p. 228.
68. Ibid., *OTS*, p. 168.
69. Ibid., *NTS*, p. 110.
70. *TPP*, p. 72.

The free offer of the gospel has generated no small amount of debate in church history, especially in Scotland. James Durham in the seventeenth century, the Marrowmen in the eighteenth century, and Thomas Chalmers in the nineteenth century all made the free offer a hallmark of their ministry.

What is the free offer? The question is a natural one descending from the doctrine of God's sovereign grace towards sinners. Opponents of the free offer say that because the blessings and benefits of Christ belong only to the elect, they should be offered only to them. Proponents of the free offer say that Christ should be offered without qualification to all. M'Cheyne was clearly in the latter camp.

Notes on the free offer of the gospel fill one of M'Cheyne's seminary notebooks from 1839.[71] An 1832 notebook finds him calling the free offer 'the stamina of good preaching.'[72] The free offer of Christ's love is found throughout his pulpit ministry because he believed ministerial faithfulness depended upon it: 'A faithful watchman preaches a free Saviour to all the world. This was the great object of Christ's ministry.'[73] M'Cheyne acknowledged the difficulty in reconciling God's election with the freeness of the gospel, yet he believed both because he found both in the Bible.[74] He taught that Christ nowhere invites 'the elect' to come,[75] but everywhere invites all people to faith and repentance.[76]

How M'Cheyne employed the free offer was simple: declare Christ's desire to save sinners. He preached a crucified Christ who willingly died for sinners and now calls to all with eager love: 'The whole Bible shows that Christ is quite willing and anxious that all sinners should come to him. The city of refuge in the Old Testament was a type of Christ; and you remember that its gates were open by night and day. The arms of Christ were nailed wide open, when he hung upon the cross; and this was a figure of his wide willingness to save all.'[77]

---

71. MACCH 1.5.

72. Ibid. 1.6, p. 112. See also, M'Cheyne, NTS, p. 55.

73. MAR, p. 536.

74. M'Cheyne, NTS, p. 199.

75. Bonar, MAR, p. 329.

76. M'Cheyne, OTS, pp. 27, 54, 110, 116, 119; M'Cheyne, SOH, pp. 85-86; M'Cheyne, TPH, pp. 178, 295; M'Cheyne, TPP, p. 171; Bonar, MAR, pp. 327, 536, 546.

77. Ibid., TPH, p. 295.

To be used of God, preachers do not need more personality or rhetorical ability. M'Cheyne believed the heralding of Christ's 'free love is all you need.'[78] When Christ's love saturates the sermon, the message is a sharp arrow that the Spirit can use to strike through sin's armor. He declared at St. Peter's: 'The free offer of Christ is the very thing that pierces you to the heart. You hear that He is altogether lovely – that He invites sinners to come to Him – that He never casts out those who do come.'[79]

The free offer was not only a doctrine to preach, but a truth to sing in M'Cheyne's ministry. One of his best-known hymns confesses,

> When free grace awoke me, by light from on high,
> Then legal fears shook me, I trembled to die;
> No refuge, no safety in self could I see, –
> Jehovah Tsidkenu my Saviour must be.
>
> My terrors all vanished before the sweet name;
> My guilty fears banished, with boldness I came
> To drink at the fountain, life-giving and free, –
> Jehovah Tsidkenu is all things to me.[80]

A fair summary, then, of M'Cheyne's theology is the knowledge of God's free love in Christ. Looking upon the Savior's unmerited love for sinners undergirds his theology. The covenant is all about the Savior's love. The Triune God's work always points to Christ's love. 'Nothing is more wonderful than the love of Christ'; hence everyone must 'learn the freeness of the love of Christ.'[81]

## Conclusion

Robert Murray M'Cheyne was no theological innovator. He had no 'new theology' to proclaim. The milk and meat of the Westminster Standards was his food, and he feasted on such doctrine all his days. His harmony with the *Westminster Confession of Faith* is best seen in how his preaching reflects the *Confession*'s chapters 'Of God's

78. Bonar, *MAR*, p. 461.
79. Ibid., p. 370.
80. Ibid., *MAR*, p. 583.
81. M'Cheyne, *TPH*, p. 168.

Eternal Decree,' 'Of God's Covenant with Man,' and 'Of Christ the Mediator.' Sovereign, covenantal, and Christ-centered love permeated his preaching ministry.

Covenant theology was the strong foundation that grounded his preaching, and rooted all his proclamations in Jesus Christ, who is the cornerstone. Christ's love for sinners was the constant note heard in his theology. He once declared, '*The love of Christ! Such is our precious theme! Can we ever weary of it? Its greatness, can we ever know? It's plenitude, can we fully contain?*'[82]

In addition to his commitment to the covenant, M'Cheyne was a thoroughgoing Calvinist. His major doctrinal tenets were the Father's sovereignty, human depravity, the Son's beauty, and the Spirit's efficacy. All four parts collided together in his catalytic preaching of Jesus Christ – the Savior freely offered to all mankind. William Garden Blaikie has captured the essence of M'Cheyne's theology best by saying that he 'brought into the pulpit all the reverence for Scripture of the Reformation period; all the honour for the headship of Christ of the Covenanter struggle; all the freeness of the Gospel offer of the Marrow theology; all the bright imagery of Samuel Rutherford; all the delight of the Erskines.'[83]

---

82. Ibid., *NTS*, p. 137 (emphasis original).
83. Blaikie, *The Preachers of Scotland*, p. 294.

# CHAPTER 4

# M'Cheyne and Loving Christ

MOST people remember Robert Murray M'Cheyne as a living monument to personal holiness. And rightly so. His blood-earnest prayer was, 'Make me as holy as a pardoned sinner can be made.'[1] No believer prays such a prayer unless he is one who pants for God (Pss. 42:1; 63:1).

Yet, to understand M'Cheyne merely as a man devoted to personal holiness, as many in history have, does not go deep enough. It is akin to noticing the beauty of a crystal-clear ocean from afar. If you remain at a distance, you get a true glimpse of the water's majesty. However, you still have not seen its fullness. If you move closer, eventually floating atop the water, you can look down and discover that the sea bursts with more life and beauty than you ever thought.

Such is the case with M'Cheyne's view of holiness. There is a depth and breadth to his understanding of Christlikeness that is often missed. We need to understand the reasons why he was so zealous for piety. Uncovering these truths will help us see why his spirituality is a model worth investigating and – ultimately – imitating.

To recover the full-orbed natured of his teaching on piety, we must consider (1) his grammar for holiness and (2) his pillars for holiness.

---

1. Bonar, *MAR*, p. 160.

## The Grammar of Holiness

Every pastor has a favorite book of the Bible. Typically, that book either had a crisis-like experiential force in the pastor's life or it resonates unusually with the pastor's disposition and personality. A simple look at M'Cheyne's extant sermon manuscripts seems to suggest Isaiah, Psalms, and Song of Songs jockeyed for the prominent place in his heart. He preached from Isaiah more than any other Old Testament text, at least thirty-two times. In second place is Psalms, from which we have twenty-two manuscripts. Song of Songs comes in third place with twelve manuscripts. Sheer numbers, however, do not tell the whole story.

One scholar writes: 'M'Cheyne's favorite Old Testament book was the Song of Solomon, whose terms and pictures constantly found their way into his preaching of Christ.'[2] The conclusion is correct. Titles and phrases from the Song of Songs show up everywhere in his sermons, diary, and letters. The Bible's love song became his anthem of holiness.

We begin to see its significance for M'Cheyne when we notice his candidating sermon at St. Peter's. His chosen text for the 14 August 1836 sermon was Song of Songs 2:8-17. The young pastor began with a broadside: 'There is no book of the Bible which affords a better test of the depth of a man's Christianity than the Song of Solomon,' he declared.[3] He went on to say:

> [If a man] hath felt his need of [Christ], and been brought to cleave unto him, as the chiefest among ten thousand, and the altogether lovely, then this book will be inestimably precious to his soul; for it contains the tenderest breathings of the believer's heart toward the Saviour, and the tenderest breathings of the Saviour's heart again towards the believer.[4]

This test for piety may appear outdated, but at least it is clear: what one thinks of the Song of Songs shows one's understanding of Jesus Christ. Making sense of M'Cheyne's piety begins with the Song of Songs. The Song was his guide for spiritual grammar and vocabulary in describing the pursuit of holiness.

---

2. Yeaworth, p. 200.
3. Bonar, *MAR*, p. 8.
4. Ibid., p. 438.

## A Parable about Christ and the Church

Many Christians today chuckle at the old notion of the Song of Songs portraying the loving communion between Christ and the church. Yet, M'Cheyne stood with countless others in church history who assumed a more allegorical reading. He belonged to a centuries-long stream of Christological interpretation that included many giants of the faith: Bernard of Clairvaux, John Calvin, and Theodore Beza. His most eminent influences approached the Song in a Christ-centered fashion: Samuel Rutherford, John Owen, Jonathan Edwards, and Thomas Chalmers.

M'Cheyne called the Song a spiritual 'parable' of the believer's communion with Christ. He delighted in Chalmers' prayer whenever reading the Song: 'My God, spiritualize my affections. Give me to know what it is to have the intense and passionate love of Christ. ... Give me, O Lord, to love Christ both for what He is in Himself and for His love to me. May His love to me constrain me to love Him back again. I long for mutual and confiding intercourse.'[5]

Experiential warmth, more than exegetical rigor, fills his instruction on the Song. His comments on the various texts were always brief and chaste. Any sermon on the Song spent most of its time explaining and applying the text's spiritual sense – the communion between Christ and an individual Christian. His sermon on Song of Songs 2:3-4[6] illustrates this typical approach. The sermon's main doctrine, developed from the verses, is that 'the believer is unspeakably precious in the eyes of Christ, and Christ is unspeakably precious in the eyes of the believer.'[7] After briefly commenting on the text's meaning, he exposits the passage under two headings: (1) what Christ thinks of the believer, and (2) what the believer thinks of Christ. Applications abound in the sermon. Few spiritual conditions go unaddressed. By the sermon's end, the people heard their pastor's central cry: 'Everything you need is in Christ.'[8] Those six words ably summarize his passionate piety.

---

5. Chalmers, 3:251.

6. 'As the apple tree among the trees of the wood, so is my beloved among the sons. I sat down under his shadow with great delight, and his fruit was sweet to my taste. He brought me to the banqueting house, and his banner over me was love (KJV).'

7. Bonar, *MAR*, p. 311.

8. Ibid., p. 316.

## A Spirituality of Loving Communion

M'Cheyne's delight in the Song surely stemmed, in part, from his affectionate personality. He resonated with the Song's tones of love, and they became hallmarks of how he spoke about spirituality. What better way is there, he asked, to talk about the Christian life than as communion between Christ and the believer? He looked to the Song for words to describe the nature of piety: 'In seasons when Christ reveals himself afresh to the soul, shining out like the sun from behind a cloud, with the beams of sovereign, unmerited love – then no other words will satisfy the true believer but these, "My beloved is mine, and I am his."'[9]

More than many realize, his pursuit of holiness was akin to a spiritual romance. He taught that the Christian is united to Christ by 'chains of love' and grows in Christ by 'melt[ing] under his love.'[10] A Christian should understand Christ as supreme Savior and loving bridegroom. He is always wooing His bride. He is always looking for His church in the secret places of grace. The Lord's heart towards His people is one of incomprehensible love. Therefore, nothing is more central to the Christian life than living in the knowledge of Christ's love.

M'Cheyne emphasized Christ's loving pursuit of the believer because

> Love is the best decider of casuistry. It is like the needle pointing to the north. Men without a compass may guess which is north and which is south, sometimes right, sometimes wrong, but he that hath the needle can say where is north. So love always points to God and doth his will. The believer loves Jesus and therefore the way of holiness is a plain one to him.[11]

'The way of holiness' meant using the ordinary means of grace – the Word, sacraments, and prayer. Previous studies on M'Cheyne's piety focus on *how* he used these means. Such an approach is appropriate; I will examine his use of the channels of grace in due course. However, a proper study of his piety begins with a more foundational query: '*Why* did he so diligently pursue Christ through the means of grace?' The answer is profound for two reasons. First, it grounds piety 'in Christ Jesus, who became to us wisdom from God, righteousness,

---

9. Ibid., p. 445.
10. Ibid., pp. 344 and 339. See also M'Cheyne, *TPH*, p. 233; M'Cheyne, *TPP*, p. 230.
11. M'Cheyne, *TPP*, p. 54.

sanctification and redemption' (1 Cor. 1:30). Second, it reveals his singular contribution to biblical spirituality. His passion for godliness, while expressed in winsome and pithy ways, is not as distinctive as many suppose. He thought his example of holiness was only a sparkle compared to the brilliance of Jonathan Edwards, David Brainerd, and Henry Martyn. While his passion for personal holiness is not unique, his rationale for pursuing holiness is distinct.

What then is the answer to why M'Cheyne stressed growth in holiness through the means of grace? The answer comes from the Song. He saw the means of grace as the primary pathways for loving communion between Christ and His people. Nothing better illustrates this idea than his preference for speaking of the means of grace as 'trysts' – secret meetings between lovers.

A sampling of his sermons shows his distinct emphasis:

> In the daily reading of the Word, Christ pays daily visits to the soul. In the daily prayer, Christ reveals himself to his own in that other way than he doth to the world. In the house of God Christ comes to his own, and says: 'Peace be unto you!' And in the sacrament he makes himself known to them in the breaking of bread, and they cry out: 'It is the Lord!' These are all trysting times, when the Savior comes to visit his own.[12]

> The Sabbath is Christ's trysting time with his church. If you love him, you will count every moment of it precious. You will rise early and sit up late, to have a long day with Christ.[13]

> The hour of daily devotion is a trysting hour with Christ, in which he seeks, knocks, and speaks and waits.[14]

> The Lord's Table is the most famous trysting place with Christ.[15]

> The sacraments especially, how sweet to the Christian – wells of salvation, Bethels, trysting-places with Christ! What sweet days of pleasure, love, and covenanting with Jesus![16]

---

12. Ibid., *TPH*, pp. 232-33.
13. Ibid., *TPP*, p. 330. See also M'Cheyne, *SOH*, pp. 32-33.
14. Ibid., *TPH*, p. 234.
15. Ibid., p. 234.
16. Ibid., p. 103.

> [Lord's Day worship] is a trysting place with Christ. It is the audience chamber where he comes to commune with us from the mercy-seat.[17]

> We love everything that is Christ's (word, prayer, sacrament, fellowship) …. We love his House. It is our trysting-place with Christ, where he meets with us and communes with us from off the mercy-seat.[18]

Referring to the means of grace as trysts highlights the centrality of Christological love in M'Cheyne's spirituality. Holiness begins when a Christian understands and believes the love of Jesus Christ. Spirit-wrought union with Christ then overflows into a life of communion between the Savior and the sinner-turned-saint. Holiness increases as the believer returns love to Christ by praying, reading God's Word, and partaking of Christ in the Lord's Supper. M'Cheyne was keen that his congregation remember the means of grace are just that – *means,* not *ends,* for godliness. Knowing Christ is the treasure of all-surpassing worth (Phil. 3:8-10). Thus, Christ is the end-goal of the means. 'Now, it is quite right to make the most diligent use of means – ministers and Bible and Christian friends; but then you must fix your eye on Christ through them all,' he explained.[19]

The trysting nature of holiness further underscores holiness as a divine romance. A passion for holiness only comes from a heart that pants for more of Christ's love. Said another way, holiness is the mature expression and highest experience of love for Jesus. To know Christ's love is to be made holy. To grow in Christ's love is to increase in holiness. Piety then, begins and ends, in a communion of Christological love.

When M'Cheyne's spirituality is seen this way, it makes sense why he turned to the Song of Songs so often. The book bursts with words and phrases for a communion of love. He panted after Christ in his diary, writing, 'Rose early to seek God, and found him whom my soul loveth. Who would not rise early to meet such company?'[20] He counseled other Christians in his letters: 'I do trust you are seeking hard after him whom

---

17. Ibid., *TPP*, 28.
18. Ibid., p. 33.
19. Ibid., p. 61.
20. Bonar, *MAR*, p. 21. He had in mind Song of Songs 3:4, which states, 'I found him whom my soul loveth.' See also Bonar, *MAR*, p. 172.

your soul loveth.'[21] He wrote to another: 'If you cannot say, "I found him whom my soul loveth," is it not sweet that you can say, "I am sick of love"?'[22]

## M'Cheyne's Portrait of Piety

In 1842, M'Cheyne published a tract titled, *Another Lily Gathered*. The slim book was his final publication. The work's subtitle reveals its purpose: *Being a Narrative of the Conversion and Death of James Laing*. Just as Jonathan Edwards illustrated his ideal spirituality in editing *The Diary of David Brainerd*, so does *Another Lily Gathered* function as M'Cheyne's model for holiness in miniature.

The Lord awakened James Laing while, at the age of eleven, the boy heard the revival sermons shaking Dundee in 1839. M'Cheyne recounts how Laing struggled to trust in Christ. 'Sometimes during the reading and prayer in the family, the word of God was like a fire to him, so that he could not bear it.'[23] In such moments, Laing departed quickly to be with his wild friends so as to drown out the cries of his convicted conscience.

Laing's day of salvation came in October of 1841. The boy's health was failing, and he was, as M'Cheyne wrote, 'intensely anxious about the salvation of his soul.'[24] He spent the entire afternoon and evening in prayer, eager to close with Christ. Late in the night he asked, 'Have I only to believe that Jesus died for sinners? Is that all?' He was told, 'Yes.' Laing then rejoiced, 'Well, I believe that Jesus died for me, for I am a poor hell-deserving sinner. I have been praying all this afternoon, that when Jesus shed his blood for sinners, he would sprinkle some of it upon me, and *he did it*.'[25]

M'Cheyne's telling of Laing's conversion reminds us how the famous preacher understood conversion: it meant coming to Christ in faith and repentance, and regularly took place in a moment of spiritual crisis.

---

21. Ibid., p. 282. See also Bonar, *MAR*, pp. 404, 405, 421; M'Cheyne, *NTS*, pp. 145-46, 303-04; M'Cheyne, *OTS*, p. 41; M'Cheyne, *TBJ*, p. 47; M'Cheyne, *TPH*, pp. 116, 117, 215, 235, 466.
22. Ibid., p. 287.
23. Ibid., p. 506.
24. Ibid., p. 507.
25. Ibid., p. 508 (emphasis original).

What is more instructive in the tract is how he evaluates Laing's godliness. He systematically shows how Laing trusted in God's sovereignty, found Christ's righteousness 'always sweet,' knew his need for the Holy Spirit, fought against temptation, loved to think on the deep things of God, sang constant praise, enjoyed secret prayer, spoke evangelistically to his friends, and – significantly – feasted on the Song of Solomon. On the last point, M'Cheyne wrote that Laing 'was very fond of the Song of Solomon, and many parts of it were opened up to him.'[26] M'Cheyne notes how he often read portions of the Song to Laing, and that the child loved to meditate on what it revealed of Jesus Christ. James' piety was summarized in a statement he made to his pastor: 'I would like to be *near* Jesus. I could not be happy unless I was near him.'[27]

In Laing, M'Cheyne found a living portrait of everything he considered to be hallmarks of holiness. Knowing that readers would wonder if the tract was hagiographical, he announced: 'I have with religious care refrained from embellishing, or in any way exaggerating, the simple record of God's dealings with this boy.'[28]

*Another Lily Gathered* illustrates M'Cheyne's belief that when God gives the grace of godliness to a soul, a soul-consuming and heart-ravishing love for Christ inevitably follows. Temptations and struggles will abound. But the Christian life 'will evermore realize and delight in the rich and glorious mystery' of Jesus Christ.[29]

## The Pillars of Holiness

As M'Cheyne read God's Word and lived in God's world, he formulated three pillars of holiness for pursuing Christ: (1) the necessity of holiness, (2) the power for holiness, and (3) the crucible of holiness.

### The Necessity of Holiness

M'Cheyne knew the Bible's teaching on holiness. The Father chose His people in Christ before the foundations of the world that they

---

26. Ibid., p. 509.
27. Ibid., p. 509.
28. Ibid., p. 521.
29. Ibid., p. 521.

would be holy (Eph. 1:4). Jesus told His people to demonstrate their love by obeying His commands (John 14:5). God's grace appeared in Jesus Christ and trains the church to grow in godliness (Titus 2:11-12). Seeking holiness is required to see God (Heb. 12:14). Therefore, holiness in Christians is normal – and necessary.

'I trust you feel real desire after complete holiness,' M'Cheyne exhorted a church member. 'This is the truest mark of being born again.'[30] In preaching and in print, he never wavered on the demand for more likeness to Christ. Sometimes his counsel was blunt. 'My friend,' he warned, 'you are no believer if Jesus hath never manifested Himself to your soul in your secret devotions.'[31] Only those who desire holiness will pursue holiness by meeting Christ in secret. A lack of devotional discipline reveals a lack of desire, which ultimately shows a lack of conversion.

More often than not, however, M'Cheyne's calling for holiness is winsome and lovely. 'May you and I be kept abiding in the Beloved to the end – nothing else is worth possessing,' he encouraged Eliza.[32] 'Oh to be like Jesus!' he cried. 'This is heaven, wherever it be. I think I could be happy among devils, if only the old man were slain in me, and I was made altogether like Jesus!'[33]

A double motive to grow in Christ energized M'Cheyne. He knew that without increasing holiness he should not be considered a Christian. He also believed unusual Christlikeness was needed as a pastor, lest he be disqualified for the office. After all, the apostle declares in 2 Timothy 2:21 that the 'sanctified (KJV)' minister is the one who is 'meet for the master's use (KJV).' Thus, M'Cheyne exhorted a newly-ordained preacher: 'Oh! study universal holiness of life. Your whole usefulness depends on this. Your sermon on Sabbath lasts but an hour or two – your life preaches all the week.'[34] He similarly encouraged William Burns: 'Oh, cry for personal holiness, constant nearness to God, by the blood of the Lamb. Bask in his beams – lie back in the arms of love – be filled with the

---

30. Ibid., p. 248. See also M'Cheyne, *TPH*, p. 43.
31. Ibid., p. 488.
32. M'Cheyne, *FL*, p. 57.
33. Bonar, *MAR*, p. 295.
34. Ibid., p. 365.

Spirit – or all success in ministry will only be to your own everlasting confusion. ... O to have Brainerd's heart for perfect holiness.'[35]

Many contexts and congregations fear an emphasis on personal piety. The potential for legalism or self-righteousness lurks around every corner. Would not M'Cheyne's passionate pleas for holiness endanger the souls at St. Peter's? They could have, but they did not.

St. Peter's readily listened and responded to his urging after holiness. Surely the supreme reason for their readiness to hear was his obvious sincerity. His genuine longing for holiness was magnetic. His appeals were not the clanging gongs of hypocrisy. No one could say with integrity that he was a man of masked spirituality. His authentic godliness amazed even his closest friends. Andrew Bonar remembered how sincerity was ever-present in M'Cheyne's life: '[Personal holiness] was never absent from his mind, whether he was at home in his quiet chamber, or on the sea, or in the desert. Holiness in him was manifested, not by efforts to perform duty, but in a way so natural, that you recognised therein the easy outflowing of the indwelling Spirit.'[36] Robert Candlish remarked: 'I can't understand M'Cheyne; grace seems to be natural to him.'[37]

However natural grace was to M'Cheyne, it is clear that he was never satisfied with his degree of personal holiness. He had a holy discontentment with his maturity in Christ. Such a dissatisfaction is itself a mark of godliness. A redeemed heart wants a greater portion of Christlikeness. It pants after the Lord and craves new sightings of the Savior. Such holy passion flowed from M'Cheyne, as he confessed, 'I earnestly long for more grace and personal holiness, and more usefulness.'[38]

Perhaps nothing illustrates M'Cheyne's longing better than his ten-page *Reformation*. Like his historical heroes – especially Jonathan Edwards – his *Reformation* contains his resolutions for personal holiness. It was written in late 1842 or early 1843. He apparently meant to add to it in the months to come. He did not get the opportunity.

---

35. Ibid., p. 250.

36. Ibid., pp. 94-95.

37. Quoted in Marjory Bonar, *Reminiscences*, p. 10.

38. Bonar, *MAR*, p. 146.

Nonetheless, the short document exudes a thirst for living water. The work has two sections. In the first, M'Cheyne focuses on 'Personal Reformation,' where he admits,

> I am persuaded that I shall obtain the highest amount of present happiness, I shall do most for God's glory and the good of man, and I shall have the fullest reward in eternity, by maintaining a conscience always washed in Christ's blood, by being filled with the Holy Spirit at all times, and by attaining the most entire likeness to Christ in mind, will, and heart, that it is possible for a redeemed sinner to attain to in this world.[39]

The proceeding pages offer a plan for increased communion with Christ that pursues confessing sin, reading Scripture, applying Christ to the conscience, being filled with the Spirit, growing in humility, fleeing temptation, meditating on heaven, as well as studying specific Christological subjects. His summary plea was, '"Make me Christ-like in all things," should be my constant prayer.'[40]

In the second section, M'Cheyne wrote on 'Reformation in Secret Prayer.' He resolved to emphasize all aspects of prayer – adoration, confession, thanksgiving, and intercession – he believed the last two areas were particular struggles in his life; he knew that to forget thanksgiving is a natural 'tendency of the heart,'[41] and he also believed vainglory in the heart prohibited intercession. Thus, his remedy was to intercede regularly for no less than twenty-five different groups or agencies. He longed to make prayer his daily priority because he believed it is the minister's 'noblest and most fruitful employment, and is not to be thrust into any corner.'[42]

## The Power for Holiness

M'Cheyne knew the means of grace contained no *ex opere operato* power for holiness. Merely reading the Bible or partaking of the Supper did not guarantee growth in godliness. Only the exalted Christ, indwelling His people by the Spirit through faith, can empower holiness. 'Remember,

---

39. Ibid., p. 151.
40. Ibid., p. 157.
41. Ibid., p. 157.
42. Ibid., p. 159.

then, my unbelieving friends, the only way for you to become holy is to become united to Christ,' he preached in a sermon on John 14:6. 'And remember you, my believing friends, that if ever you are relaxing in holiness, the reason is, you are relaxing your hold on Christ. Abide in me, and I in you; so shall ye bear much fruit. Severed from me, ye can do nothing.'[43]

Union with Christ is the fount of holiness. One way to think about M'Cheyne's Christ-centered approach to the means of grace is to see them as channels of love. In the Word, Christ speaks to His people. In the sacraments, Jesus kisses them. In prayer, believers return love to Him. Love is thus the energetic force motivating holiness. He explained, 'If Christ's love to us be the object which the Holy Ghost makes use of, at the very first, to draw us to the service of Christ, it is by means of the same object that he draws us onwards, to persevere unto the end.'[44] The Spirit loves to woo the believer with one constant argument: Christ's love.

Exalting Christ's role in holiness by no means shuns the Spirit. 'The love of Christ to man, continually present to the mind by the Holy Ghost,' M'Cheyne declared, 'should enable any man to live a life of gospel holiness.'[45] Personal piety grows as the Christian gazes on Christ, but only the Spirit can enable such sight. Increased holiness is always an exercise in utter dependence on the Spirit.

M'Cheyne knew that ordinary Christians tend to minimize the Spirit's work and power. In early 1839, he was away from St. Peter's for an extended time recuperating from illness. A church member asked him for a weekly pastoral letter to encourage the flock. He quickly put pen to paper. In his fifth pastoral note, he spoke about a common tendency in the church: 'The most of God's people are contented to be saved from the hell that is *without*. They are not so anxious to be saved from the hell that is *within*. I fear there is little feeling of your need of the indwelling Spirit.'[46] He saw this trend in his own heart and comments in the *Reformation*: 'I ought to study the Comforter more –

---

43. Ibid., p. 303.
44. M'Cheyne, *TPH*, p. 53.
45. Ibid., pp. 47-48.
46. Bonar, *MAR*, p. 198 (emphasis original).

his Godhead, his love, his almightiness. I have found by experience that nothing sanctifies me so much as meditating on the Comforter, as John xiv. 16. And yet how seldom I do this!'[47] There is no holiness without the Spirit. Yet, how many Christians unintentionally train themselves for godliness without Christ's Spirit?

Union with Christ and reliance on the indwelling Spirit is the energy for godliness. There is one more key in M'Cheyne's program for piety. It is a pillar that many overlook.

## The Crucible of Holiness

Suffering is the sandpaper God uses to increase the shine of holiness. Hardships refine, trials deepen, and affliction strengthens faith. M'Cheyne's peculiar way of discussing communion with Christ arrives when he discusses suffering in the Christian life. 'Afflicting time is trysting time,' he asserts.[48] A careful survey of his sermons shows he often emphasized the blessing of hardship. He taught that God sends affliction to 'open the heart.' Once opened, the Spirit leads us to see Christ more clearly, to learn of His love, to feel His comfort, to know His presence, to sense His sympathy, to be assured of His grace, and to pray to Him.[49] 'Afflictions,' he held, 'are sweet to the taste' of every true believer.[50]

Personal experience provided M'Cheyne countless occasions to reflect on God's providence in affliction. Sickness constantly took him away from St. Peter's. He believed God sent the suffering to chasten and to teach. Self-examination gave him many reasons to repent and renew obedience. He was thus able to bless God through affliction. While at the Divinity Hall, he even prayed for hardship lest God leave him to secret sin. 'If nothing else will do to sever me from my sins,' he prayed, 'Lord send me such sore and trying calamities as shall awake me from earthly slumbers. It must always be best to be alive to thee, whatever

---

47. Ibid., p. 155.

48. M'Cheyne, *TPH*, p. 491.

49. Ibid., p. 117.

50. Ibid., *TPP*, p. 45; M'Cheyne, *TPP*, p. 68; M'Cheyne, *NTS*, p. 98; M'Cheyne, *BOF*, p. 134; M'Cheyne, *TPH*, p. 519; M'Cheyne, *TBJ*, p. 101; M'Cheyne, *TPH*, p. 472; M'Cheyne, *TPH*, p. 416; M'Cheyne, *TPH*, p. 335; M'Cheyne, *TPH*, pp. 162, 79; *SOH*, pp. 53, 61, 165; M'Cheyne, *OTS*, p. 29; M'Cheyne, *TPH*, p. 117; Bonar, *MAR*, p. 316.

be the quickening instrument.'[51] An openness toward suffering was an early feature of his piety. He knew that suffering is God's choice academy for learning Christ. He exhorted: 'Let affliction strike heavy blows at your corruptions, your idolatries, and self-pleasing and *worldly schemes*. Learn much of Christ at such an hour.'[52]

## Christlikeness in the Whole Man

From head to toe, and heart to hand, our members are meant for Christ. The Westminster Shorter Catechism defines sanctification as 'the work of God's free grace, whereby we are renewed in the whole man after the image of God, and are enabled more and more to die unto sin, and live unto righteousness.'[53] Godliness should be evident in all our faculties, words, and deeds.

One of the more celebrated features of M'Cheyne's life was his whole-person conformity to Christ. He ached for such a reality. 'Oh for closest communion with God, till soul and body – head, face, and heart – shine with divine brilliancy! but oh for a holy ignorance of our shining!'[54] His internal love for Christ led to an external brilliance that struck friends and strangers alike. In all the memorials left after his death, a consistent theme arises: when preaching Christ, his manner was more striking than his method or message.

M'Cheyne preached his final sermons at St. Peter's on 12 March 1843. He lay in bed the next week with typhus fever, never to recover. A letter was delivered that week and placed on his desk. It went unopened until after his death: 'I hope you will pardon a stranger for addressing you a few lines,' the letter began. 'I heard you preach last Sabbath evening, and it pleased God to bless that sermon to my soul. It was not so much what you said, as your manner of speaking, that struck me. I saw in you a beauty in holiness that I never saw before.'[55]

The stranger struck the heart of M'Cheyne's genuine holiness: it was all consuming. In every place, he exuded Christlikeness. One would

---

51. Bonar, *MAR*, pp. 25-26.
52. Ibid., p. 272 (emphasis original).
53. *WSC*, p. 35.
54. Bonar, *MAR*, p. 131. See also, Bonar, *MAR*, p. 27; *TPH*, p. 81.
55. Quoted in Bonar, *MAR*, pp. 162-63.

notice it in his morning devotions, his leading of family worship, his conversations on the street, his visitation in the parish, his prayers, and his preaching – even his holy singing was a marvel to many! His piety was entire and always public.

Isabella Dickson, Andrew Bonar's eventual wife, wrote after hearing M'Cheyne preach: 'There was something singularly attractive about Mr. McCheyne's holiness .... It was not his matter nor his manner either that struck me; it was just the living epistle of Christ – a picture so lovely, I felt I would have given all the world to be as he was.'[56] Over and over, the reports of his evident godliness sounded forth. His holy conduct left its stamp at evangelistic campaigns, preaching stations, and revival meetings. When he ministered in Jedburgh, 'the impression left was chiefly that there had been among them a man of peculiar holiness. Some felt, not so much his words, as his presence and holy solemnity, as if one spoke to them who was standing in the presence of God; and to others his prayers appeared like the breathings of one already within the veil.'[57]

The Christian life, for M'Cheyne, is one of complete and continual growth in Jesus Christ. His was not an ethereal holiness; it was embodied holiness. True holiness is an all-consuming passion for Christ. A person who grows in godliness will increasingly think like Christ, speak like Christ, feel like Christ, react like Christ, and love like Christ. Entire likeness to Christ – devotion in the whole man – is the aim of biblical piety.

## Conclusion

Complete conformity to Christ is something that tends to astound the world – even other Christians. So it was with M'Cheyne. Grace seemed natural to him. Yet, his life and doctrine show nothing is natural about the Christian life. It is utterly supernatural. It is the story of a sovereign grace poured into a sinner's heart, grace that allows one to see God's glory in the face of Jesus Christ. Christ's glory is His loveliness. For the converted heart, such a sight is ravishing. Like Peter on the Mount of

---

56. Bonar, *Robert Murray M'Cheyne*, p. viii.
57. Ibid., *MAR*, p. 138.

Transfiguration, a believer wants to set his tent in the Son's presence, delighting always in the King's beauty and majesty.

The central lesson, then, that M'Cheyne's passion for holiness teaches is that love for Christ is the ordinary expression of piety. Communion with Jesus is the supreme joy, the highest pleasure, and all-surpassing delight of a redeemed soul. M'Cheyne summed up his vision for godliness in a letter he wrote to his parents in March of 1837: 'Let us be glad in all that God gives so richly to enjoy – and use all for him. If we are all his children, washed in the blood of his Son, led by his Holy Spirit, [let us live] a life of prayer and reading of the word and growing in likeness and nearness to him.'[58]

---

58. MACCH 2.1.10.

# PART 3:
# A Ministry of Holiness

# CHAPTER 5

# M'Cheyne and Growing in Christ

EVERY Christian tradition offers unique emphases in its doctrine of sanctification. The most noted feature of Reformed and Presbyterian piety is, arguably, its emphasis on using the means of grace for holiness.

The Westminster Larger Catechism asks, 'What are the outward means whereby Christ communicates to us the benefits of his mediation?' It answers: 'The outward and ordinary means whereby Christ communicates to his church the benefits of his mediation, are all his ordinances; especially the word, sacraments, and prayer; all which are made effectual to the elect for their salvation.'[1]

The means of grace are ordinary channels the Spirit uses to bring Christ to His people. M'Cheyne agreed, reminding the St. Peter's congregation that the ordinances 'are the channels through which God pours His Spirit. The Bible, prayer, the house of God – these are the golden pipes through which the golden oil is poured.'[2] He also liked to speak of the means of grace as 'wells of salvation.'[3] The Word, sacraments, and prayer are indeed the living waters of truth and grace. At such wells, we enjoy the all-satisfying ocean of Christ's love.

M'Cheyne loved to think of these channels, pipes, and wells as trysts between Christ and the Christian. It is through the means of grace that Christ

---

1. Westminster Larger Catechism 154.
2. Bonar, *MAR*, p. 210.
3. M'Cheyne, *TPH*, p. 219.

begins his regular visits to the soul. In the daily reading of the Word, Christ pays daily visits to sanctify the believing soul. In daily prayer, Christ reveals himself to his own in that other way than he doth to the world. In the house of God Christ comes to his own, and says: 'Peace be unto you!' And in the sacrament he makes himself known to them in the breaking of bread, and they cry out: 'It is the Lord!' These are all trysting times, when the Saviour comes to visit his own.[4]

In and through the means of grace we not only experience Christ's love, we also express love to Christ. Let us learn what we can from M'Cheyne practices of communion with Christ.

## Growing through God's Word

M'Cheyne had an intense and almost insatiable appetite for God's Word. He considered the Bible sweeter than honey and more precious than rubies. An immediate consequence of his conversion in 1831 was that he 'began to seek God to his soul, in the diligent reading of the Word.'[5]

While studying at the Divinity Hall, he made a goal of reading daily twenty-verses in the Bible's original languages (Hebrew and Greek). One of his college notebooks offers six resolutions for studying God's Word:

> *Read it regularly.* Set apart an exact time for it.
>
> *Read in more places than one.* Thus, a historical piece and a devotional psalm, a piece of a gospel and a piece of an epistle.
>
> *Read with parallels.* Either 2 or 3 verses. Or the most difficult parts, or the most interesting.
>
> *Read whole books.* A whole epistle, or little prophet, and trace and overlook the divisions into chapter and verse.
>
> *Try to understand.* Ask where you do not.
>
> *Pray before and after.* In devotional parts turn every verse into prayer.[6]

His normal practice once he was ordained was to read three chapters a day, taking notes as the Spirit led. He would then review the previous week's

---

4. Ibid., pp. 232-33.
5. Bonar, *MAR*, p. 8.
6. MACCH 1.7 (emphases original).

readings on the Lord's Day. His correspondence often speaks of what he was learning in personal study. For example, he wrote to Alexander Somerville: 'I have been reading the Book of Acts with great delight and encouragement…. I have been reading also the 119th Psalm, with meditation. I love to muse over it, and seek that it may be engrained in my heart.'[7]

M'Cheyne's hunger for God's Word was large enough that, in 1837, he created a Bible reading plan that got him through the whole Bible in one month. It's not clear how often he did this, but it would have meant reading about fifty chapters each day.

Perhaps the most striking – and moving – comment M'Cheyne made related to Bible reading is found in a letter he wrote to Horatius Bonar just months before dying. 'I love the Word of God, and find it sweetest nourishment to my soul. Can you help me to study it more successfully?' he asked.[8]

The request came when M'Cheyne was at the summit of his ministry. His renown was great. His influence was singular. At this time, he could be heard leading presbyters in a stirring prayer at the evangelical Convocation of 1842. And, yet, he wanted help in studying his Bible. He wanted more skill so he could be more successful. How many Christians and well-known pastors today express such desire to get a better harvest in the fields of Scripture?

M'Cheyne not only asked for help in studying God's Word, he also counseled others in the same. 'You read your Bible regularly, of course,' he wrote to a young seeker, 'but do try and understand it, and still more, to *feel* it. Read more parts than one at a time. For example, if you are reading Genesis, read a psalm also; or, if you are reading Matthew, read a small bit of an Epistle also.'[9] He exhorted in a sermon: 'Learn to search the Scriptures; to lie down in these green pastures; to drink from those still waters. Take up your Bible with prayerful uplifted eyes. Turn its threatenings into confession; as dew draws out the odour from the flowers, so will the Holy Spirit draw out the fragrance of heaven from this garden of delights.'[10]

---

7. Smith, *A Modern Apostle*, p. 35.
8. Bonar, *MAR*, p. 274.
9. Ibid., p. 48.
10. M'Cheyne, *TPP*, p. 273.

M'Cheyne's lasting legacy in the area of Bible reading is his congregational reading plan, 'Daily Bread,' written in 1842 for St. Peter's and still used around the world. The scheme guides readers, on average, through four chapters a day. If followed entirely, a Christian will read through the New Testament twice, the Psalms twice, and the rest of the Old Testament once per year.

The reason why Christians delight in reading God's Word is because it is nothing less than an encounter with Christ. The Bible is not merely a record of God's work in history; it is the revelation of Jesus Christ. M'Cheyne asked, 'Sometimes, when reading the Bible alone, has not the voice of Christ been louder than thunder?'[11] The young preacher's eagerness to study Scripture was so strong because he met Christ on the sacred page. The whole Bible testifies of Jesus Christ. His shadow and substance fill every page. Therefore, M'Cheyne proclaimed:

> Spread out the record of God concerning His Son. The gospels are the narrative of the heart of Jesus, of the work of Jesus, of the grace of Jesus. Spread them out before the eye of your mind, till they fill your eye. Cry for the Spirit to breathe over the page, to make a manifested Christ stand out plainly before you; and the moment that you are willing to believe all that is there spoken concerning Jesus, that moment you will wipe away your tears, and change your sighs for a new song of praise.[12]

M'Cheyne's logic for constant Bible reading went like this: Christians meet the Savior in Scripture, and the green pastures of glory await every soul who sits before revealed truth, looking for and listening to Christ. Who would not journey to these fields of grace? As one of M'Cheyne's hymns on Psalm 119:105 sings,

> O grant in me thy Word to see
> A risen Saviour beckoning me.[13]

Sustained study of Scripture gives vitality to biblical piety. 'Go then,' he exhorted, 'to Jesus for all you need; learn the means of sanctification – the Word. No holiness without the Bible!'[14] He also declared, 'Unless

---

11. Bonar, *MAR*, p. 327.
12. Ibid., p. 334.
13. Ibid., p. 591.
14. M'Cheyne, *BOF*, p. 54.

you love your Bibles, and feed upon them, you will never stand with the Lamb upon Mount Zion, with golden harps.'[15]

## Growing through the Sacraments

The Westminster Confession of Faith teaches that 'There be only two sacraments ordained by Christ our Lord in the Gospel; that is to say, baptism, and the Supper of the Lord.'[16] Baptism is the sacrament of initiation into the covenant body of Christ, whereas the Lord's Supper is the sign of covenant ratification – the Table is where God confirms His promise and feeds His people with Christ.

### Baptism in the Christian Life

M'Cheyne's writings do not contain any substantial teachings on baptism; brief comment and anecdote are more typical. He was a committed paedobaptist, believing the New Covenant sign belongs to believers and their children. More often than not, his teaching on baptism was corrective. Andrew Bonar recalls a time when M'Cheyne forcefully refused to baptize an infant because he believed the parents were presenting the child out of mere superstition. On another occasion, he wrote to his parents: 'Saw the Baptismal service (at Hampstead) – far too long – too many kneelings, and the absurd signing with the cross on the forehead of the child. The sponsors, too, seemed ignorant clowns.'[17]

One common spiritual threat he faced was the congregation's false views of baptism's power. He decried how many in Dundee come to the Lord's Table 'to get baptism for your child.'[18] In other words, Christians came to the Supper not to commune with Christ but to show outward devotion to the Lord that allowed the ministers to receive the children as worthy recipients of covenant baptism.

M'Cheyne did offer positive instruction on baptism, particularly to students. He advised young communicants (those children baptized at a younger age and soon to partake of the Lord's Supper for the first time) to come to the Table looking back on their 'baptism with a soothing

---

15. Ibid., p. 55.
16. *WCF* 27.4.
17. M'Cheyne, *Familiar Letters*, p. 12.
18. Ibid., *TPH*, p. 389. See also M'Cheyne, *TPH*, p. 219; M'Cheyne, *TPP*, p. 203.

complacency,' remembering that they are the Lord's and the Lord is theirs,[19] for God makes covenant promises to His children in baptism.[20] He also taught families that baptism is not a physical rite, its true meaning is spiritual: 'Baptism [is] not merely external washing, but real and internal, signifying and sealing our union with Christ.'[21] Further, his baptismal form explained how baptism signifies 'the gift of the Holy Ghost ... [who] purifies from all corruptions the heart of all them that believe.'[22]

The blessings that baptism promises are only received through faith. Baptism does not automatically effect faith, nor does it guarantee future faith. The sacrament, as a sign and seal of God's promise, calls the recipient to faith. He reminded his church, 'Without faith on the part of the baptized the mere washing with water is of no avail.'[23]

## The Lord's Supper in the Christian Life

If baptism is a river of truth in M'Cheyne's world of spirituality, the Lord's Supper is an ocean. Preparing the church for communion and preaching during communion seasons occupied him for months each year. He called the Supper 'the sweetest of all the ordinances.'[24] Jesus is the center of the meal. 'Christ is the Alpha and Omega of the Lord's Supper; it is all Christ and Him crucified. These things have a peculiar sweetness to the broken bread and poured-out wine.'[25]

When M'Cheyne arrived at St. Peter's, the church planned to celebrate the Lord's Supper twice a year. He quickly moved to administer the Supper at least four times a year. Such frequency was a novelty at the time in the Church of Scotland.

The Lord's Supper was distributed during a long week of gatherings, which was collectively known as the 'communion season.' The excitement began on the Lord's Day a week before the sacrament was received – so seven days in advance. The following Thursday consisted of two 'Fast

---

19. Ibid., p. 154.
20. Ibid., p. 134.
21. Ibid., *NTS*, p. 117. See also M'Cheyne, *TPH*, p. 158. See also, *WCF* 28.1.
22. MACCH 3.2.16.
23. Ibid.
24. Bonar, *MAR*, p. 522.
25. Ibid., p. 522.

Day' services for prayer and humiliation. Friday and Saturday each held a special service to further prepare the people. On Sunday, the day of communion, the elements were typically distributed from 1:00 p.m. to 7:00 p.m. The supper began with one minister preaching the 'Action Sermon,' which usually highlighted Christ's loving welcome to weary sinners. After urging action, the minister then gave a brief address on 'Fencing the Table.' M'Cheyne's message in such moments was to invite all repenting sinners to come, and to come with appropriate reverence and solemnity.

The fencing complete, small groups of communicants assembled at a table located at the front of the church. The minister then offered short comments on the gospel meal before distributing the elements. Late in the evening, when everyone had been served, M'Cheyne concluded the day with another short homily that provided specific Scriptures for meditation. Monday was called 'The Day of Thanksgiving' and a corresponding worship service happened. Because the following Lord's Day almost invariably mentioned the previous Sunday's communion, all told, the Lord's Supper occupied no less than twelve Sundays each year at St. Peter's.

M'Cheyne loved communing with Christ at the Table. He regularly extolled the Supper as a meeting time with Jesus, saying, 'The broken bread and poured-out wine represent the broken body and shed blood of Christ. Oh, it is enough to melt the heart of the stoutest to look at them!'[26] In keeping with his confessional convictions, he knew the Supper was more than a memorial of Christ's death on the cross. He called it 'an appropriating act'[27] in which we 'do feed on Christ.'[28]

M'Cheyne's Song-of-Songs-shaped heart infused his statements about the Supper. He spoke of the sacrament as a feast for the soul, a time when believers enter the Lord's banqueting house and find their hearts burning in love for Him. 'The Lord's Table is the most famous trysting-place with Christ,' he stated. 'It is then that believers hear him knocking, saying: "Open to me."'[29]

---

26. Ibid., p. 432. See also M'Cheyne, *TPH*, p. 191.
27. Ibid., p. 523. See also Bonar, *MAR*, pp. 525-26.
28. M'Cheyne, *BOF*, p. 62.
29. Ibid., *TPH*, p. 324.

In many churches today, the sacraments are sideline celebrations. In other churches, there is a renewal of emphasis on the sacramentality of baptism and the Lord's Supper. The ordinances are rightly understood as one way the Lord signifies and seals Christ to His people. To be baptized is to receive the Lord's promise. To feast at the Supper is to revel in God's promise – and Christ Himself. With M'Cheyne, then, we announce, 'The sacraments especially … [are] trysting-places with Christ! What sweet days of pleasure, love, and covenanting with Jesus!'[30]

## Growing through Prayer

Prayer is the lifeblood of spirituality. God speaks to us through His Word, and we speak back to Him through prayer. Prayer is thus faith made audible.

It is entirely impossible to overstate the priority of prayer in the pursuit of Christ. M'Cheyne called prayer the Christian's 'noblest and most fruitful employment.'[31] Secret prayer meant everything to him because it was the Savior's deepest pleasure. 'Christ loved secret prayer,' he explained. 'Ah, you are no Christian, if you do not love secret prayer. O brethren! a prayerless man is an unconverted man.'[32]

Sadly, we have no record of M'Cheyne's actual prayers. We do not know their structure. We do not know their passion. We do not know their content. However, we do know much about his practice of prayer. He was ardent in prayer – both privately and publicly.

M'Cheyne aimed to start each day with prayer. His goal was to be out of bed by 6:30 a.m. so he could spend two hours in prayer and meditation. If ministry demands shortened the time, he resolved to dress hurriedly and spend at least a few minutes alone with God. 'In general,' he wrote in his *Reformation*, 'it is best to have at least one hour *alone with God*, before engaging in anything else.'[33] M'Cheyne's Sabbath prayers were more strenuous. He set aside six hours for prayer and Bible reading.

M'Cheyne longed for balance in his secret prayer, to engage in confession, adoration, thanksgiving, petition, and intercession. The *Reformation* lists no less than twenty-eight categories of individuals

---

30. Ibid., p. 103.
31. Bonar, *MAR*, p. 159.
32. M'Cheyne, *BOF*, p. 49.
33. Bonar, *MAR*, p. 158.

and groups for whom he should pray. One of his prayer diaries lists the following subjects for intercession:

## Prayer List 1: People

*Relations*: home/William/Hunters/Dicksons/cottage.

*Friends:* Macgregors/Grahams – Lizzy/Sommer/Bonars/Campbells/Thain.

*People:* careless/anxious (followed by a list of names)/Brought to peace (eighteen names listed)/Christians (included a list of ruling elders and their districts).

*People:* Female club/young men's club/young communicants/Sabbath Schools (at least three mentioned)/the sick (twenty names recorded).

*Dying:* three names.

That God would raise up elders and Sabbath School teachers and prayer meetings.

Preached word on Sabbath/visitation/preached word on week evening/prayer meeting/small prayer meetings.

*Ministers:* Friends, young ministers, all ministers in Dundee/Edinburgh/the land. All missionaries – India (three names)/China/Africa. Against Popery/Jews ('Here I am send me. Thy kingdom come.')

Those suffering persecution.

## Prayer List 2: Subject Headings

For an abundant gift of the Holy Spirit.

For the purity and unity of the Church of Christ.

For her majesty the Queen and all in authority under her and for a special blessing upon our country.

That God may raise up in great numbers fit persons to serve in the ministry of his church.

That a blessing may accompany the ministrations of the Word of God, in order that it may have free course and be glorified.

For the propagation of the gospel among the heathen.

For the fulfilment of God's promises to his ancient people.

For a special blessing on all the members of the Assembly and Church.[34]

---

34. Quoted in Robertson, *Awakening*, pp. 130-31.

In addition to private prayer, M'Cheyne championed prayer gatherings. He led a Saturday prayer meeting in Thomas Chalmers' vestry while at the Divinity Hall. He created a ninety-minute prayer meeting for Dundee pastors on Monday mornings. This meeting was an invitation-only gathering. He wrote to Horatius Bonar, 'Of course, we do not invite the colder ministers; that would only damp our meetings.'[35] He also started monthly prayer meetings for like-minded ministers throughout Scotland. They would set aside a day, typically the first Monday of the month, for prayer on keeping their life and doctrine pure. The ministers involved took turns writing the monthly prayer letter, which reminded the brothers of the upcoming prayer day and offered thoughts and subjects that were suited for the time.

M'Cheyne and St. Peter's also participated in the Church of Scotland's called-for prayer days. St. Peter's was one of the first congregations in Scotland to host monthly prayer meetings focusing on the Church's future – a suggestion from the 1840 Assembly. In 1841, St. Peter's joined a ten-day 'Prayer Union Service' happening in churches throughout the land. At least eight hundred people gathered every morning at 8:00 a.m. during the special season.

The most important prayer meeting, for St. Peter's, was the weekly Thursday night gathering. M'Cheyne believed they were meetings that would 'doubtless be remembered in eternity with songs of praise.'[36] As many as eight hundred people met each Thursday. M'Cheyne began by reading a Scripture and commenting briefly on how it related to the prayer time. He normally focused on the person and work of the Holy Spirit. After a time of prayer, he read a story of revival from church history. Perhaps, then, it is no surprise that revival fell on Dundee – they prayed for it earnestly and perpetually. St. Peter's theme could be described as, 'Oh, give us more of the Spirit, more of His power, and more of His reviving grace!'

M'Cheyne's prayer life was no pietistic performance. His devotion was sincere. At the Convocation of 1842, he offered a proposal for united prayer throughout the nation. Soon the meeting's debate over

---

35. Bonar, *MAR*, pp. 119-20.
36. Ibid., p. 63.

the church's future became tense. He led the hundreds of attendees in prayer following the discussion. One person recorded, 'The spirit of prayer ... from the lips of Mr M'Cheyne ... conveyed a profounder sense of the divine presence than we ever felt before or since in the most hallowed of our Christian assemblies.'[37] Because his parish ministry was always packed, someone asked him if the demands minimized time for prayer. He was dumbfounded: 'What would my people do if I were not to pray?'[38]

M'Cheyne demanded a measure of prayer in ministers that can seem excessive today. He cried, 'If a minister is to thrive in his own soul, and be successful in his work, he must be the half of the time on his knees.'[39] He would not trust a man's call to ministry if it did not manifest itself in devoted prayer. Preachers, he believed, needed to set their priorities aright – and prayer came first. 'Prayer is more powerful than preaching. It is prayer that gives preaching all its power.'[40] A ministry that mirrors apostolic priorities will spend the first half of its time in prayer.

While it is true that M'Cheyne expected ministers to be extra devoted to private prayer, he still called for a noticeable commitment among ordinary Christians. Recall the quote above: 'Christ loved secret prayer. Ah, you are no Christian, if you do not love secret prayer. O brethren! a prayerless man is an unconverted man.'[41] The emphasis here on 'love' is central in M'Cheyne's mind. Yes, secret prayer is a duty. But a truly redeemed heart will grow to a point where prayer is its chief delight. It is through prayer that 'the soul enjoys great nearness to God, enters within the veil, [and] lies down at the feet of Jesus.'[42]

Personal prayer is thus a trysting time with Jesus Christ. The Savior loves to meet His people in the prayer closest. Channeling the Song of

---

37. Stewart J. Brown, p. 335.
38. Bonar, *MAR*, p. 51. See also Bonar, *MAR*, p. 547.
39. M'Cheyne, *BOF*, p. 119.
40. Ibid., *TPH*, p. 83. M'Cheyne also exhorted ministers to consider the example of Paul: 'O that all ministers could pray like Paul. Probably no man ever lived who was the means of saving so many souls as Paul. Probably no minister was ever made the instrument of bringing his people to such a height of holiness as Paul. How was this? Look at his prayers for an answer' (M'Cheyne, *HTD*, p. 50).
41. Ibid., *BOF*, p. 49.
42. Ibid., *TPH*, p. 419.

Songs 2:17, M'Cheyne asked, where is 'spring-time of love, Immanuel coming over the mountains of Bether?'[43] The answer: secret prayer.

## Conclusion

M'Cheyne's personal piety has captivated Christians throughout the ages. What continues to lie at the center of his model, for many believers, is his devotion to the means of grace. He satisfied his almost insatiable hunger and thirst for righteousness at 'the wells of salvation': the Word, sacrament, and prayer. If we peer deep enough into his program, however, we will see the real pulsating power for his godliness – love for Christ.

M'Cheyne knew it is possible to make a Christ out of the means of grace. We can make our 'quiet time' or 'devotional hour' the end of our pursuit. A proper biblical spiritually understands the means of grace are precisely that, *means*. Communion *with Christ* is the end. Thus, M'Cheyne counseled,

> Increase thy diligence in the means of grace. If you have truly found the Lord Jesus, be often at the spot where you have met with Him. If you have found Him in the Word, be faithful and diligent in meeting Him there. If you begin to let your Bible slip, you are beginning to let Jesus slip. If you found Him in secret prayer, give more earnest heed to meet Him often there. It is a sweet-trysting place with Jesus, 'within the vail.' If you let slip the throne of grace, you let Him slip who sits thereon. Have you found Jesus in the sanctuary, then 'love the habitation of his house, and the place where his honour dwelleth' (Ps. 26:8). Has he revealed Himself to you in the breaking of bread, then 'continue steadfastly in the apostles' doctrine, and in fellowship, and in breaking of bread, and in prayer' (Acts 2:42).[44]

M'Cheyne's unique contribution to the pursuit of holiness is how the means of grace are 'trysts' with Christ. Jesus speaks to us in love through His Word. The sacrament is a mutual exchange of love as the Savior gives Himself to us and we feed on Him by faith. We speak back in love to Christ through prayer. Thus, the means of grace are indeed meetings of love, where the soul cries, 'I am my beloved's and He is mine.'

---

43. Ibid., *HTD*, p. 5.
44. Ibid., *HTD*, p. 80.

CHAPTER 6

# M'Cheyne and Preaching Christ

ROBERT Murray M'Cheyne was a herald of Jesus Christ. Many remember him for his pursuit of holiness, missionary labors, or revival experiences. He, however, understood himself to be – first and foremost – a preacher. Preaching is the minster's 'grand business.'[1] He also reminded, 'As weak and foolish as it may appear, [preaching] is the grand instrument which God has put into our hands, by which sinners are to be saved, and saints fitted for glory.'[2]

Why then is M'Cheyne rarely included in the nineteenth century's hallowed homiletical halls, alongside portraits of Charles Spurgeon, Charles Simeon, and Archibald Alexander?

His short life is surely one reason. His sermonic catalog is not as expansive nor as mature as it would have been, had he lived another five decades. Another reason is the printed medium cannot capture his brilliance in the pulpit. Even his contemporaries recognized this. Alexander Moody-Stuart, himself a renowned preacher during M'Cheyne's time, revealed, 'Many of M'Cheyne's hearers would have thought that the effect of his preaching was partly owing to the halo effect of interest attaching to himself, and that *his words would lose not a little when committed to print*; but they are more powerful when read

---

1. Bonar, *MAR*, p. 360.
2. Ibid., p. 360.

and when dissevered from all that was adventitious.'[3] In other words, M'Cheyne's preaching does not translate well to books of sermons. Andrew Bonar likewise wrote:

> It is difficult to convey, to those who never knew him, a correct idea of the sweetness and holy unction of his preaching. Some of his sermons, printed from his own manuscripts, may convey a correct idea of his style and mode of preaching doctrine. But there are no notes that give any true idea of his affectionate appeals to the heart and searching applications. These he seldom wrote; they were poured forth at the moment when his heart filled with his subject.[4]

One modern biographer believes M'Cheyne's '"success" cannot be gleaned from published written material, much of which will only appeal to those who already are convinced of his "sainthood".'[5] In truth, few preachers' successes will ever be seen in their written manuscripts. Preaching is a momentary, auditory, and physical event. A particular pathos infuses every sermon. Whatever emotions boom from the pulpit, they never transfer perfectly to the printed page. And yet, the fact that M'Cheyne's sermons continue to be printed almost two hundred years since their delivery show there must be something special in his preaching. To read his full sermon manuscripts out loud is to hear his heart on display: Love for Christ is the sweetest theme.

If we are to understand M'Cheyne's preaching program, we must consider not just how he constructed and delivered sermons. We must first notice how he embodied the apostolic ideal – preaching Christ crucified in the power of the Spirit.

## Resolving to Preach Christ

M'Cheyne was ordained on 24 November 1836. His chosen text for his first sermon as minister of St. Peter's was Isaiah 61:1-3, with a focus on 61:1: 'The Spirit of the Lord God is upon me; because the Lord hath anointed me to preach good tidings (KJV).'

The text was precious to M'Cheyne. He returned to it each year to commemorate his start in Dundee. The last time he preached from it

---

3. Moody-Stuart, pp. 49-50 (emphasis added).

4. Bonar, MAR, p. 65.

5. Robertson, Awakening, pp. 127, 191.

was in November of 1842. On that date he told St. Peter's: 'The more anointing of the Holy Spirit, the more success will the minister have.'[6] Thus, from the start, dependence on the Spirit was the posture of his preaching. He did not expect any success apart from the Spirit's blessing. He also had no hope of blessing if his preaching did not exalt Jesus Christ.

The ordination festivities on 24 November 1836 ended with a formal dinner at Campbells Hall Hotel. Sixty guests were present. Toasts and speeches were made. M'Cheyne's address to the dinner party was the climax of the night. Standing assured, but somewhat unclear of how to best serve the audience after a day full of spiritual joy, he resorted to his place of comfort. He declared that he came to St. Peter's with one desire: to proclaim 'Christ and Him crucified.' He then closed the meeting by reminding his fellow believers that 'the presence of the Lord is the true glory of every church.'[7] No pastorate should aim at another ideal. The Lord dwelling with His people – through His Word and Spirit – is the aim of a faithful ministry. Preaching is the means to reach that goal. According to M'Cheyne, preaching Christ in the power of the Spirit is the beginning, middle, and end of a faithful ministry.

The young minister possessed enormous gifts. His character was winsome and full of charm. It is thus striking to discover how absent his persona was in the event of preaching. He did not build a church or establish influence on the authority of personality. Nor did he trust in his native ability to reach the masses. He preached in utter reliance on the Holy Spirit. His favorite picture of the Spirit's anointing came from Zechariah 4 and the prophet's vision of the golden lampstand standing next to two olives trees. Employing his typological hermeneutic, M'Cheyne understood the trees to represent gospel preachers. The word to Zechariah was the word to every minister: 'Not by might, nor by power, but by my Spirit, says the Lord of hosts' (Zech. 4:6). Every preacher must therefore pray to 'be filled with the fire of the Spirit, that you may pierce into the hearts.'[8]

---

6. Bonar, *MAR*, p. 530.
7. Quoted in Van Valen, p. 147.
8. Bonar, *MAR*, p. 365.

Because the Spirit comes to exalt Jesus Christ (John 16:14), M'Cheyne knew a Spirit-anointed preacher would be a Christ-centered preacher. He announced, 'Preach Christ for awakening, Christ for comforting, Christ for sanctifying.'[9] The apostle Paul reminded the Colossians how Christ lay at the center of true ministry when he wrote, 'Him we proclaim' (Col. 1:28). Gospel preaching is not a presentation about Jesus Christ; it is the proclamation of Christ. Andrew Bonar thought M'Cheyne preached in the apostolic spirit: 'It was not *doctrine* alone that he preached; it was *Christ*, from whom all doctrine shoots forth as rays from a centre. He sought to hang every vessel and flagon upon him.'[10]

M'Cheyne did not shy away from preaching the whole counsel of God. His sermon manuscripts offer a catalog of messages that span the canon. He left no section or genre of Scripture untouched. Yet, for M'Cheyne, nothing compared to preaching Christ directly. He wrote in his diary after a sermon on Revelation 1:15: 'It is strange how sweet and precious it is to preach directly about Christ, compared with all other subjects of preaching.'[11]

## How M'Cheyne Preached Jesus Christ

M'Cheyne lived in an era that craved preaching. His was an age when, as one scholar says, 'the old evangelical sermon' thrived.[12] Such a sermon accented Jesus Christ with the language of conversion, piety, and revival – typical of nineteenth-century evangelicalism. The day's demand was for radical religion in the heart. M'Cheyne stepped into this homiletical context possessing the gifts needed to reach the hearts of his hearers.

Three things are necessary to know when evaluating M'Cheyne's preaching: (1) the interpretive method of his exegesis, (2) the homiletical tools he used for constructing his sermon, and (3) his style of delivery. The final point is arguably his greatest contribution to preachers today.

### M'Cheyne's Method of Biblical Interpretation

M'Cheyne's interpretive method was not original. He exegeted Scripture like hundreds of evangelical Scottish ministers in the 1830s. He learned

---

9. Ibid., p. 361.
10. Ibid., p. 65 (emphasis original).
11. Ibid., p. 65.
12. Enright, pp. 207-12.

his method at the feet of Thomas Chalmers. One word summarizes Chalmers' hermeneutical scheme: doctrinal.

Students received a three-pronged hermeneutical method from Chalmers: the philological, the contextual, and the doctrinal. The philological element parsed the original words and phrases of sacred Scripture, noticing the grammar of tenses and moods. The contextual facet examined the chosen text in its immediate and canonical context. For all practical purposes, Chalmers paid little attention to the first two interpretive components. He instead maximized the text's doctrine. He told aspiring preachers that the essential question when preparing sermons was not, 'What does this text mean?' but, 'What doctrine does this text preach?'[13] Thus, Chalmers' approach – and the one used by M'Cheyne – leaned into systematic theology. It was less concerned with exegetical particulars; what mattered most was the main doctrinal truth in the text.

Agreeing with the Common Sense philosophy of his time, Chalmers taught: 'The very utterance of your text will generally be enough for gaining their assent to the doctrine which it enunciated. … I would curtail the formal proof of a doctrine.'[14] The idea was this: the congregation would – almost always – easily understand the text's essential truth. The preacher should not belabor the obvious. Application and exhortation, more than explanation, should make up the bulk of a sermon.

M'Cheyne adopted his mentor's method. Extant sermon manuscripts show how he typically began with a few exegetical comments before stating the main doctrine of his text. The rest of his sermon then wove subsequent exposition in and through Christ-centered applications.

A second feature of M'Cheyne's interpretive method was his deep love of typology. A type is an event, person, or institution in Scripture that serves as an example for other events, persons or institutions. One modern theologian offers a definition that captures M'Cheyne's method: Typology 'is a hermeneutical concept in which a biblical place (Jerusalem, Zion), person (Adam, Melchizedek), event (flood, brazen serpent), institution (feasts, covenant), office (prophet, priest, king), or object (tabernacle, altar, incense) becomes a pattern by which later

---

13. See Enright, pp. 234-36.
14. Quoted in Enright, p. 238.

persons or places are interpreted due to the unity of events within salvation-history.'[15]

One need only read through the collection of M'Cheyne's sermons from Hebrews to see how typological his preaching was.[16] He ransacked the Bible for types of Christ. He focused on many well-known types: Abraham's offering of Isaac, the Passover Lamb, the Bronze Serpent, the temple. He also emphasized other lesser known types such as the Old Testament cities of refuge and the two olive trees in Zechariah. His notebooks contain a commentary on twenty different types of Christ.[17] Although M'Cheyne ordinarily spoke on Christological types, he also elaborated on other doctrinal types representing the covenant of grace, the devil, the church, the Holy Spirit, eternal rest, and Pentecost. So pervasive was his typological outlook that a sermon on Christ's healing of the deaf and mute man became an extended commentary on how the event is a 'type of the way in which Jesus saves a poor sinner.'[18]

M'Cheyne's doctrinal-typological approach was his hermeneutic for preaching Christ. Applying Common Sense philosophy to his homiletics, he rarely sought to defend or prove a doctrinal or typological point. He instead took such truths as obvious. The majority of his sermon intended to drive the truth home to the congregation's soul and every person's conscience.

## M'Cheyne's Method of Constructing Sermons

Clarity was M'Cheyne's style of sermonic construction. He aimed for simple language and heart-searching analogies. His sermon followed a long-esteemed pattern of (1) announcing the text's main doctrine, (2) illuminating the doctrine along a series of headings, and (3) applying the sermon as broadly as possible – with the most striking appeals reserved for the end. Although he had many mentors in this method, it appears that David Welsh was singularly important. 'I used to despise Dr Welsh's rules at the time I heard him,' M'Cheyne admitted, 'but now I feel I *must*

15. Grant Osborne, 'Type, Typology,' in *The International Standard Bible Encyclopedia*, edited by Geoffrey W. Bromiley (Grand Rapids: Eerdmans, 1979), 4:930.

16. See M'Cheyne, *SOH*.

17. M'Cheyne, *TPP,* pp. *90-120.*

18. Ibid., *NTS*, pp. 42-51.

*use* them, for nothing is more needful for making a sermon memorable and impressive than a logical arrangement.'[19] A friend of M'Cheyne mentioned his memorable divisions, recalling, 'The heads of his sermons were not the mile stones that tell you how near you are to your journey's end, but they were nails which fixed and fastened all he said. Divisions are often dry; but not so *his* divisions – they were so textual and so feeling, and they brought out the spirit of a passage so surprisingly.'[20]

M'Cheyne believed diligent study was necessary for a sermon to be clear. Vague preaching tends to come from little meditation on the passage – and on the planned exposition. He critiqued Andrew Bonar's habit of sounding unclear, telling his friend, 'Study to express yourself very clearly. I sometimes observe obscurity of expression. Form your sentences very regularly. ... It sometimes strikes me you begin a sentence before you know where you are to end it, or what is to come in at the end.'[21]

M'Cheyne's attentive and deliberate preparation did not result in sermons overflowing with insincere, polished rhetoric. As James Dodds recalled,

> On several occasions I heard Mr M'Cheyne preach in Edinburgh; and I can testify to the singular earnestness and unction of his ministrations. He never aimed at high argument or eloquence, or anything very profound or original. ... His extraordinary spirituality and earnestness, the elegance of his action, and the simple beauty of his language, soon overcame all prejudices, and deeply impressed every hearer that had any discernment or love of spiritual things. His views of the Gospel truth were full and clear; his deep knowledge of Scripture was manifest in almost every sentence he uttered; and his acquaintance with the human heart was wonderfully complete in one so young.[22]

Preachers often think a deep, logical argument will persuade the congregation. High-sounding words may be impressive, but they rarely

---

19. Bonar, *MAR*, p. 29 (emphasis original).
20. Ibid., p. 64.
21. Quoted in Marjory Bonar, *Reminiscences*, p. 7.
22. Dodds, p. 77. Dodds knew M'Cheyne from his time at Ruthwell and remembered that his earliest attempts behind the pulpit were 'full of fine fancy and Hebrew learning.' In time and with maturity, M'Cheyne's language 'became plainer' (Dodds, p. 75).

strike with power. As M'Cheyne knew, more often than not, the Spirit uses simple announcements of Christ to awaken a soul. 'It is the truth of God in its naked simplicity,' he instructed, 'that the Spirit will honour and bless.'[23]

## M'Cheyne's Method of Sermon Delivery

M'Cheyne's method of sermon preparation offered little, if anything, novel. Yet, in the arena of sermon delivery he made a lasting contribution. 'The new element he brought to the pulpit, or rather which he revived and used so much that it appeared new, was *winsomeness*,' William Blaikie concluded.[24] Tenderness dripped from M'Cheyne's pulpit ministry. Herein lies the secret of his success in preaching. For most of his hearers, he embodied the dove-like qualities of the Holy Spirit and the lamb-like sympathies of Jesus Christ.

A personal lament M'Cheyne recorded during his first year of ministry underscores his aim to preach Christ with tenderness. 'Large meeting in the evening,' he wrote. 'Felt very happy after it, though mourning for *bitter speaking of the gospel*. Surely it is a gentle message, and should be spoken with angelic tenderness, especially by such a needy sinner.'[25] On another occasion, he wrote: 'Preached with some tenderness of heart. Oh, why should I not weep, as Jesus did over Jerusalem?'[26]

M'Cheyne's emphasis on tenderness does not mean his preaching was 'weak.' Meekness is not weakness. In fact, the flip side of his typical delivery was an unrelenting urgency. He was always pushing, pleading, and exhorting. He critiqued much contemporary preaching as weak on pleading:

> I would observe what appears to me *a fault in the preaching of our beloved Scotland*. Most ministers are accustomed to set Christ before the people. They lay down the gospel clearly and beautifully, but they do not urge men to enter in. Now God says, Exhort, – beseech men, – persuade men; not only point to the open door, but compel them to come in. Oh to be more merciful to souls, that we would lay hands on men and draw them in to the Lord![27]

---

23. Bonar, *MAR*, p. 361.
24. Blaikie, pp. 294-95 (emphasis original).
25. Bonar, *MAR*, p. 169 (emphasis original).
26. Ibid., p. 39.
27. Ibid., p. 362 (emphasis original).

Life is short. Tomorrow is not promised. Thus, every encounter with God's Word was one that happened on the precipice of eternity. M'Cheyne sought to reflect the apostolic ideal of 2 Corinthians 5:20: 'Therefore, we are ambassadors for Christ, God making his appeal through us. We implore you on behalf of Christ, be reconciled to God.' He pursued a preaching ministry that invited sinners with tenderness, wooed the weary with gentleness, *and* compelled the congregation to find their seat at the Lamb's wedding feast.

As his ministry developed, M'Cheyne came to believe that preaching without notes was the ideal method for the urgently tender preaching of Christ. His argument for preaching without substantial pulpit helps shows how much his convictions changed over the years.

The preaching instruction M'Cheyne received at the Divinity Hall emphasized writing out a full sermon manuscript. One seminary notebook finds him observing: 'The extemporaneous is a good temptation to indolence and is apt to lead you always into the same strain of preaching. The bulk of your parish preparations should be in writing, but in a rapid style of writing.'[28] His earliest sermons embodied what he learned at seminary. He wrote a complete manuscript and then memorized its substance, so it never appeared as if he was reading the text. When he was nominated to St. Peter's several people wanted to know if he read his sermons. The people clearly wanted a preacher who labored with freedom from the pulpit. They were delighted to discover that he was not in the habit of reading sermons.

The providential event that moved M'Cheyne to preach without notes came one Lord's Day. As he rode rapidly along to Dunipace, his written sermons fell on the wayside. This accident prevented him from having the opportunity of preparing in his usual manner; but he was enabled to preach with more than usual freedom. For the first time in his life, he discovered that he possessed the gift of extemporaneous composition, and learned, to his own surprise, that he had more composedness of mind and command of language than he believed.[29]

---

28. MACCH 1.6, p. 107.
29. Bonar, *MAR*, p. 38.

The extant material shows how much shorter his sermon manuscripts became over time. His outlines reflect his constant concern for order and clarity. Part of the reason for his smaller manuscripts is due to the increased number of preaching opportunities after 1839. Also, the more a pastor preaches, the less he needs external aids. His confidence grows, his understanding of Scripture is sharper, and his biblical recall is like a library at his fingertips.

Therefore, after only a few short years of preaching, M'Cheyne espoused a model of sermon delivery that leaned on diligence by the Spirit in the study and dependence on the Spirit in the pulpit.

## What M'Cheyne Preached about Christ

M'Cheyne's preaching ministry was all about looking. He meant for his hearers to look on Jesus Christ and live. As Moses lifted the bronze serpent in the wilderness, so did M'Cheyne raise the Savior in every sermon. He believed, 'Faithful ministers preach Jesus Christ as Lord.'[30] Beholding Jesus Christ is the goal of all preaching.

One recent study concludes that the evangelical preachers of M'Cheyne's day emphasized soteriology at the expense of Christology.[31] His preaching shows the falsehood in such a dichotomy. Christological preaching is inescapably soteriological, for we preach the Christ who died for sinners. Thus, M'Cheyne could urge: 'Preach Christ for awakening, Christ for comforting, Christ for sanctifying.'[32] He preached a whole Christ to the whole church. His sermon catalog shows his preaching program emphasized, with particular verve, Jesus Christ as Surety, Savior, and Judge.

### Christ the Surety

Christ as 'surety' is not a description many Christians use today. During M'Cheyne's time, it was shorthand for 'one who acts in place of another.' A surety is a guarantee or pledge to a different person. The Westminster Larger Catechism captures the truth of Christ as surety by asking, 'How is justification an act of God's free grace?' The Catechism answers:

---

30. M'Cheyne, *BOF*, p. 6.
31. Enright, p. 217.
32. Bonar, *MAR*, p. 361.

> Although Christ, by his obedience and death, did make a proper, real, and full satisfaction to God's justice in the behalf of them that are justified; yet inasmuch as God accepteth the satisfaction from a *surety*, which he might have demanded of them, and did provide this *surety*, his own only Son, imputing his righteousness to them, and requiring nothing of them for their justification but faith, which also is his gift, their justification is to them of free grace.[33]

Thus, to highlight Christ's work as surety is to focus on His forensic benefits, namely, justification and imputation. M'Cheyne summarized this part of Christ's work by saying: 'I have often explained that Christ came to be a Surety, not only in suffering for sinners, but in obeying also, obeying inwardly and outwardly the law of His Father.'[34] He once reminded St. Peter's, 'We often set forth Immanuel, the Surety of perishing sinners.'[35]

His exalting of Jesus Christ as surety meant he necessarily spent much time speaking of Christ's obedience. When Jesus cried, 'It is finished!' He announced the completion of His surety work. He achieved His mission of obedience for His people. Christ's total submission to His Father was done in the stead of sinners. Thus, to take hold of Christ by faith is to lay hold of His perfect obedience. M'Cheyne's preaching on this point also led him to revel in the joy of imputation – Christ's righteousness credited to sinners by faith. He proclaimed: 'Behold thy Surety! How fully He obeyed in your stead. Ah! cling you to Him and all the merit of His holy obedience is yours. You are complete in Him.'[36]

Jesus Christ did not only obey in our place, He also suffered for us. These twin realities are what theologians have traditionally called Christ's active and passive obedience. His 'passive' obedience refers to His suffering in our stead. M'Cheyne declared:

> Through his whole life Christ was a suffering surety, but he was especially so in his dying. Had he stood for himself he would have had no sufferings, for he knew no sin, neither was guile found in his mouth. But though he knew no sin, yet God made him to be sin for us. God made him as if he

---

33. *WLC* p. 71 (emphasis added).
34. M'Cheyne, *NTS*, p. 31.
35. Ibid., *OTS*, p. 55. M'Cheyne regularly employed 'Surety' as a title for Christ. See also, M'Cheyne, *NTS*, pp. 116, 244, 254; M'Cheyne, *OTS*, p. 93; *TPP*, p. 24.
36. Ibid., *NTS*, p. 32. See also, M'Cheyne, *NTS*, p. 134.

were all sin from head to foot. ... God charged him with the ten thousand thousand sins of all that ever had believed.[37]

An anthropological assumption drove much of M'Cheyne's preaching of Christ: man is depraved from birth. The just condemnation of death belongs to every person. Redeeming and reconciling sinners came at a price – the blood of the spotless Lamb of God.

M'Cheyne's belief about man's plight meant he necessarily proclaimed Christ as an atoning surety. Meditations and proclamations about the value of Christ's blood seep through his sermons. His focus on the blood of the lamb grew out of a soul that soaked in the typological significance of the Old Testament ceremonies. He knew that blood flowed like a torrential river in the Old Covenant. The sacrificial system announced that blood must be shed for a person to enter God's presence. Man's blood could never atone for sin – it has the vile stain and stench of iniquity. Such an offering could not grant entrance into God's holy presence. Also, the blood of sacrificial animals could not permanently stay God's wrath. Yet, 'He that offers to be your Surety,' M'Cheyne declared, 'offers to cover all your sins with His own blood.'[38] It is the blood of Christ that heals all wounds. Christ our surety erases sin 'with His bloody hand.'[39] He frequently stated how Christ's blood saves, provides entrance into God's presence, and takes away the guilt of sin forever.

Ultimately, M'Cheyne taught, Christ's work as surety uncovers God's love for sinners. He announced: 'The heart of Christ is revealed – his love to the lost, his undertaking for them, his suretyship obedience, his suretyship sufferings. Glorious Christ! Precious Christ!'[40] When a Christian grasps Christ the surety, there are abundant reasons for praise, peace, delight, confidence and rest.

## Christ the Savior

A truly gospel ministry is a converting ministry. 'Conversion,' M'Cheyne announced, 'is the most glorious work of God.'[41] He reminded his

---

37. Ibid., *TPP*, p. 198.
38. Ibid., *NTS*, p. 272.
39. Ibid., *OTS*, p. 55.
40. Ibid., *TPH*, p. 58.
41. Ibid., p. 224.

congregation, 'The great use of the ministry – engrave it on your hearts, tell it to your children – that the use of ministry is to convert your soul.'[42]

To say conversion was the preoccupation of his preaching is no overstatement. He so zealously emphasized God's work in saving souls that he eventually admitted some were 'angry that I speak so much of conversion.'[43] Nevertheless, he remained steadfast. Every sermon sought to continue Christ's mission of seeking and saving the lost. No sermon was complete until he urged children, the awakened, and the hardened sinner to look on Christ and live.

An unexpected aspect of M'Cheyne's preaching of Christ as Savior is how he applied this work of Jesus to the conscience of his church. The immediate application to the unconverted was obvious: repent and believe. But what is the ordinary application of Christ's sovereign salvation for Christians? M'Cheyne would say it is brokenhearted, evangelistic prayer.

> If you were to mingle with poor unconverted souls in the God-forgetting companies, where they dance, drink, are gay and merry, singing their own songs, and enjoying themselves in their accustomed manner, what could you expect to do for their conversion? You should weep over them, and seek their salvation, rather than let down your Christianity and join them in worldliness, forgetfulness of God, carnal mirth, and giddy folly. If you would do them good, you must seek God's Holy Spirit to give you a heart to weep for them.[44]

## Christ the Judge

The Bible is full of warnings and threats. M'Cheyne did not apologize for God's wrath towards sin. He preached regularly on the coming judgment. He was no hellfire-and-brimstone pulpit beater. Instead, he was a pastor who knew eternity awaits each hearer. The final judgment loomed on the horizon, and so every person needed to know what was coming.[45]

---

42. Ibid., *BOF*, p. 77.

43. Ibid., *TPH*, p. 349. See also, M'Cheyne, *NTS*, p. 201.

44. Ibid., *NTS*, pp. 87-88.

45. A quick study of his preaching shows how often he centered St. Peter's collective soul on Christ's coming judgment. He preached sermons with titles like, 'God's Rectitude

As with their complaints about his emphasis on conversion, some in Dundee wanted the young pastor to de-emphasize future judgment. In one sermon, he mentioned, 'Sometimes you wonder at our anxiety for you. Sometimes you say, "Why are you so harsh?" O poor soul! It is because the house is on fire. ... Every day that passes is bringing you nearer to the judgment-seat.'[46] He believed that, far from being strident on judgment, he was too light on the topic. 'Oh! I fear that many may reproach me on a death-bed, or in hell, that I did not tell you oftener that there was a hell,' he confessed. 'Would to God I had none to reproach me at last!'[47]

The reality of Christ's love even found its way into M'Cheyne's preaching of Christ as Judge. 'The deepest place in hell will be for [anyone who] is not ravished with His beauty, and attracted to Him by His loveliness,' he warned.[48]

M'Cheyne preached the full breadth of Scripture's teaching on judgment. His sermons include references to hell, destruction, misery, dread, damnation, terror, groaning and shrieking, torment, darkness, and weeping and gnashing of teeth. In light of God's judgment, the message was clear and consistent: 'Flee the wrath to come!'

A unique feature of his preaching is how often he spoke to those he termed 'almost Christians.' In a day when Christianity had much cultural cache, he knew many listeners were 'almost' through the narrow gate. Too many drew near to Christ without ever resting on Him. M'Cheyne's severest warnings went to this group. He proclaimed:

> The deepest place in hell will be for almost Christians. In strict justice it will be so. The more sin the greater guilt and the deeper hell. And who has so much sin as the soul that comes nearest to Christ, yet is not ravished with His beauty, and attracted to Him by His loveliness. In the nature of things, the hell of the 'almost Christian' will be more severe than that of others.

---

in Future Punishment' (Ps. 11:6-7); 'The Day of Great Slaughter' (Isa. 30:25-26); 'The Sword Over the Ungodly' (Ezek. 21:9-10); 'Future Punishment Eternal' (Mark 9:44); 'Enemies of the Cross' (Phil. 3:17-21); 'Do Not Provoke God' (Heb. 3:16-19); and 'The Eternal Torment of the Dead, Matter of Eternal Song to the Redeemed' (Rev. 19:3).

46. M'Cheyne, *BOF*, p. 80.
47. Ibid., p. 80.
48. Ibid., *NTS*, p. 102.

To be almost saved, and yet to be lost; to be not far from the kingdom of God, and yet to fall into the kingdom of wrath – Oh, that will be an awful thought to all eternity![49]

Perhaps nothing proves M'Cheyne's urgent tenderness in preaching as does his heralding of Christ the Judge. Sinners stood on the precipice of eternity, soon to find Christ's judgment falling on them. How could a faithful preacher not warn them? He believed loving tenderness was the required tone for preaching hell's horror. 'Learn that it is in love we beseech you,' he explained. 'Am I become your enemy, because I tell you the truth? When we speak of sins, your lost condition, the wrath that is over you, the hell beneath you, it is in love.'[50] The pastor that loves his people most is the preacher who speaks most plainly of hell. But plainness does not mean carelessness. No man can rightly preach on sin's penalty without pleas of love. Thus, M'Cheyne insisted, 'The man who speaks of hell should do it with tears in his eyes.'[51]

Jesus Christ is the Lord's servant who sustains the weary with a word. He is gentle in spirit, never breaking a bruised reed. He is humble in heart, never quenching the flickering flame. Even when preaching Christ's work as judge, gospel preachers must have the meekness of Jesus. Andrew Bonar recalled one occasion when he and M'Cheyne spoke on their previous Lord's Day sermons. Bonar's text had been Psalm 9:17, which says that 'the wicked shall be turned into hell (KJV).' M'Cheyne's immediate question was, 'Were you able to preach it *with tenderness*?'[52]

## Conclusion

Pastors are heralds of Christ. They steward and proclaim Christ's unsearchable riches. The degree to which Christ arrests the preacher's heart will be the degree to which Christ saturates sermons from that preacher. M'Cheyne's success as a preacher rested on this reality: he had comprehended the breadth, length, height, and depth of Christ's

---

49. Ibid., p. 102.
50. Ibid., p. 277.
51. Ibid., *TPH*, p. 35.
52. Bonar, *MAR*, p. 42 (emphasis original).

love. Therefore, like a dropper full of honey, his sermons dripped with Christological sweetness.

M'Cheyne's powerful preaching stemmed from two realities. First, he always aimed to exalt Christ – crucified, buried, resurrected, and glorified. Every sermon called the congregation to gaze on the King's beauty. He knew that 'the more ministers have Christ in their sermons, the more they faithfully preach.'[53] Therefore he was content to not answer every question or objection the text generated. He was in a hurry to get to Calvary. Jesus alone is the feast that satisfies the soul. Therefore, M'Cheyne aimed to preach a whole Christ to form people wholly devoted to the Savior.

Second, M'Cheyne maintained that 'Faithful ministers preach from personal experience.'[54] In ways almost ineffable, hearers sensed an unusual sincerity in his preaching. Whatever the topic, his sermon possessed a gravity of felt experience. Sometimes the experience came from the trials of life – personal suffering, sickness, and sorrow. At other times the experience came from time in the study. He emerged on the Lord's Day as a man whom the text had grabbed. The truth was a fire in his heart. The Savior was the delight of his soul. And he preached accordingly.

---

53. M'Cheyne, *BOF*, p. 28.
54. Ibid., *NTS*, p. 155.

CHAPTER 7

# M'Cheyne and Sharing Christ

THE Scottish church of the early-to-mid nineteenth century dreamed about missionary endeavors. It was the dawning of the modern missionary movement. Britain's colonial expansion, coupled with the aftershocks of the Evangelical Revival, helped organize new causes for missions. In 1796, the Church of Scotland's General Assembly received overtures calling for missionary activity in other lands for the first time. The Church's deliberate approach towards world evangelization meant activity was a few decades in the making. The culminating moment came in 1829 when, with enormous festivity, Alexander Duff departed for India as the Kirk's first missionary.

Robert Murray M'Cheyne had the missionary spirit from the start of his life in Christ. In November of 1831, just weeks after starting his studies at the Divinity Hall, M'Cheyne wrote in his diary: 'Reading H. Martyn's *Memoirs*. Would I could imitate him, giving up father, mother, country, house, health, life all – for Christ.'[1] Diary entries from the summer of 1832 show a young man still wrestling with missionary desires. He wrote on 19 May: 'Thought with more comfort than usual of being a witness for Jesus in a foreign land.'[2] In early June, he talked about a conversation he and Alexander Somerville had 'on missions' and the missionary's necessary heart condition

---

1. Bonar, *MAR*, p. 12.
2. Ibid., p. 15.

for fruitful service. On 27 June, he found inspiration in another historical figure by reading the *Life of David Brainerd*. 'Tonight, more set upon missionary enterprise than ever,' he revealed.[3] Missionary zeal continued to blow during his second year of theological study. The following summer's diary provides a longer, introspective entry on the subject:

> Why is a missionary life so often an object of my thoughts? Is it simply for the love I bear to souls? Then, why do I not show it more where I am? Souls are as precious here as in Burmah. Does the romance of the business not weigh anything with me? – the interest and esteem I would carry with men? – the nice journals and letters I should write and receive? Why would I so much rather go to the East than to the West Indies? Am I wholly deceiving my own heart? And have I not a spark of true missionary zeal?[4]

The Mission of Inquiry provided M'Cheyne a sustained glimpse at missionary life. While he never pursued a call to international missions, Andrew Bonar says his friend 'ever cherished a missionary spirit.' After struggles in Dundee, M'Cheyne admitted, 'This place hardens me for a foreign land.'[5]

What few people know is that, in the months leading to his death, M'Cheyne was working to leave St. Peter's in Dundee. He was planning to become an itinerant evangelist. William Chalmers Burns had been urging his friend to join him in the harvest. Burns wrote:

> I know not how it is, but it seems more clear to me that you must without delay give up your charge, and enter on that tempting field in which I am honoured to be. The fields are white. ... Do not wait for a *Church* call. Christ's call is better. Souls are perishing! Let us to the rescue, and leave others to abide by the *stuff*. You understand me; I do not undervalue *pastoral work*. But there must be a *spiritual* flock gathered first.[6]

Robert took his friend's counsel to heart. On 7 March 1843, just days before contracting the illness that would kill him, he told his sister Eliza, 'I think the church should give me a roving commission at once.

---

3. Ibid., p. 16.
4. Ibid., pp. 20-21.
5. Ibid., p. 84.
6. Quoted in Smellie, p. 146 (emphasis original).

I can almost say, as Wesley did to the Bishop of London ... "The world is my parish.'"[7]

That M'Cheyne would leave a fruitful ministry in Dundee to become a roving preacher indicates the depth of his evangelistic heart. Like the old Puritan Joseph Alleine, who he read, he 'was infinitely and insatiably greedy for the conversion of souls.' He once declared: 'I feel there are two things it is impossible to desire with sufficient ardour – personal holiness, and the honour of Christ in the salvation of souls.'[8] 'I think I can say,' he told in a sermon on the gospel ministry, 'I have never risen a morning without thinking how I could bring more souls to Christ.'[9]

From start to finish and in every area, M'Cheyne meant to take Christ to the masses. His evangelistic program had four features worth noting: (1) house visitation, (2) ministry to children, (3) revival, and (4) church extension.

## Evangelism through House Visitation

M'Cheyne's early models in ministry – Henry Duncan, Thomas Chalmers, and John Bonar – all pursued the priority of parish visitation. The system he learned, and eventually adapted in Dundee, ministered to every soul in the area. Home visitation was not only for members of the congregation; it was for every person entrusted to the pastor.

While at Dundee, he typically visited roughly twenty homes per day. All told, he spent six hours visiting each day except Sunday. His scheme was simple. First, he notified the family the day before he visited. The notice allowed both the family and minister to prepare. When he assisted John Bonar at Larbert and Dunipace, he wrote home of his amusement at an elder's common practice of warning a household 'the day before (visiting), so that their houses and bairns are all as clean and shining as pennies new from the mint.'[10] In time, he too valued the practice of a day-before notice of when he would knock on the door.

When M'Cheyne arrived, he first discerned the home's spiritual maturity if he did not already know it. He asked about the family's

---

7. Quoted in Smellie, pp. 146-47.
8. Bonar, *MAR*, p. 242.
9. M'Cheyne, *BOF*, p. 77.
10. MACCH 2.9.21.

religious identity. Should children be present, he asked a few questions from the Shorter Catechism. He then read a few passages from Scripture, offering relevant counsel in the remaining time. As he left, he invited the family to an evening meeting in the neighborhood. These evening services often attracted as many as two hundred people, where a neighborly spirit imbued those gathered with warmth for the coming 'cottage lecture.' His evening lectures could last as long as ninety minutes.

Ever eager to evangelize, M'Cheyne spoke to every person in the home – even guests. One of his notebooks records, 'Rules Worth Remembering,' when on visitation. The first rule is, 'When visiting a family whether ministerially or otherwise, speak particularly to the strangers about eternal things – perhaps God has brought you together just to save the soul.'[11]

'Painstaking, yet pleasurable,' is the best way to describe his visitation approach. Visitation was his favorite part of ministry while at Larbert and Dunipace. At Dundee, he most cherished preaching, but visitation was a key cog in his evangelical labor.

M'Cheyne sketched maps of various districts to ensure he could return to homes visited in the byways. His notebooks reveal immense care in record keeping. One section was devoted exclusively to the sick. He believed such a focus honored Christ who acknowledged, 'I was sick, and ye visited me.' He used certain cases of illness to exercise his interest in medicine. His older brother was a medical doctor, and M'Cheyne evidently cultivated an amateur's knowledge of medicine. He occasionally recorded 'the pulses of the sick, and even noted the symptoms and his diagnoses, mentioning such examinations as: "Listened at her back and heart and heard work of death going on fearfully."'[12] His dabbling in medicinal diagnoses caused a problem with the local doctor. One entry finds him somewhat exasperated that 'Dr. Tennant has forbidden all disturbance from ministers. So the body doctor has thrust out the soul doctor.'[13]

---

11. Ibid. 1.10, p. 29.
12. Quoted in Yeaworth, p. 159.
13. Van Valen, p. 176.

In each visitation entry, he recorded the recipient and date of visitation. He made quick comments on the home's spirituality, recording in red ink the Scripture(s) he read. A representative entry looks like this:

> Anne Moodie (House West of Millers): Nice looking, intelligent woman – sat, in chapel shade. *Visit 31, Jan. 1837*: His faithfulness in affliction – all taught of God. [She's] seemingly a woman of God – very humble and meek in appearance & affectionate. *Visit 7, Feb.*: She not better. Hosea v. Spoke plainly – tho' searching in the dark not knowing whether she be a child of God or not. *Visit 21, Feb.*: Better. Xt (Christ) the intercessor for us. Xt having prayed for us in his agony are assured that he now intercedes.[14]

M'Cheyne devoted extra attention to those near death, especially if they were children. He wrote of a young girl named Jean:

> Fine girl of eleven or twelve dying of water in head – spoke to her 1st day on the good shepherd gathering the lambs – she cautiously speaks but seems to love the word. 2nd day 23rd Psalm – much the same – asked her if she would like to lie on the shoulders of the Good Shepherd – she said yes. 3rd day – Prodigal son – she seems to listen with peace and joy. 4th day – Noah and the ark – she heard plainly. Died 23rd March 1838 – I hope in peace. When the schoolmaster had been speaking to her she said, 'I wish he could have spoken to me all night.'[15]

The visitation scheme was vast. The ruling elders helped as much as they could, especially during times of an epidemic in the parish. Like other ministers of his time in Scotland, M'Cheyne appointed deaconesses to visit widows and comfort them in their loneliness.

M'Cheyne's faithfulness in visitation is unquestioned. His fruitfulness, however, is harder to assess. His notebooks record difficulties – even debates! – during visits. For example, one entry remarks on a visit with one Thomas Fyrie who was zealous to engage him in a debate about hell and annihilation.[16] All in all, M'Cheyne proved himself content to do the ministry's work and rely on the Spirit to bring the prayed-for harvest.

---

14. MACCH 1.14.
15. Ibid.
16. Ibid.

## Evangelizing Children

Children occupied a cherished place in M'Cheyne's ministry. Young hearts were regular targets for his gospel arrows. He published a well-received tract entitled, *Reasons Why Children Should Fly to Christ*, which collected and systematized his standard teaching for children. He believed that youth is the best season for conversion. 'Youth is a day of grace,' he urged. 'If you intend to come to Jesus and be saved, there is not time so seasonable as the time of one's youth.'[17] It is in the days of youth that the heart is tender, soft, and impressionable.

> Most people who are ever converted are converted in youth. Conviction of sin and conviction of righteousness are most easily wrought into the youthful mind. ... Now, although conversion be a supernatural work, yet it is true of conversion also, that it is far oftener wrought in youth than afterwards. My young friends, this is your day of grace; remember, it quickly passes, the twilight is at hand; the night cometh when no man can believe.[18]

In addition to addressing children directly in his sermons,[19] M'Cheyne pursued creative measures to reach them with the gospel. He started a Sabbath Sunday School in 1837 – an innovation at the time in Scotland. St. Peter's also hosted a special worship service for children at 8:00 a.m. every Lord's Day. The Sabbath School met from 6:00–8:00 p.m. and quickly grew to one hundred and fifty participants. His ability in reaching children served the school well. He aimed both to entertain and to teach: 'I gather all sorts of interesting scraps to illustrate the catechism, and try to entice them to know and love the Lord Jesus,' he told his parents.[20]

---

17. M'Cheyne, *NTS*, p. 85.
18. Ibid., p. 85.
19. For examples of exhortations to children, see Bonar, *MAR*, pp. 315, 322-24, 348, 351, 397, 399, 456, 540, 570; M'Cheyne, *BOF*, pp. 67, 87, 94, 98; M'Cheyne, *NTS*, pp. 85, 198, 233, 311; M'Cheyne, *OTS*, pp. 44, 47, 49, 59, 104-05; M'Cheyne, *TPH*, pp. 25, 26, 130, 205, 229-30, 297, 349, 350, 428, 458; M'Cheyne, *TPP*, pp. 49, 85, 109, 146, 223. See also his hymns, 'Children Called to Christ' and 'The Child Coming to Jesus.' *MAR*, pp. 589, 596-97.
20. Quoted in Van Valen, p. 128.

A second strategy to reach children was the Tuesday night meeting for youth too old to attend the Sabbath School. Over two hundred and fifty students attended the Tuesday gathering. M'Cheyne's instruction focused on evangelistic Bible texts and the Shorter Catechism. The most common topic discussed on Tuesdays was the doctrine of sin. M'Cheyne explained, 'The greatest want in the religion of children is generally *sense of sin*.'[21]

To see his method, consider his Tuesday teaching from on Shorter Catechism 19: 'Q. What is the misery of that estate whereinto man fell? A. All mankind by their fall lost communion with God, are under his wrath and curse, and so made liable to all miseries in this life, to death itself, and to the pains of hell forever.'

His teaching outline flowed through three heads: (1) What we have lost; (2) What we have come under; and (3) What are we liable to. His notes represent a clear commentary on the features found in the Catechism's answer. He reminded the students that 'as children you are *all* under' God's wrath and curse. He also penned a poem to cement the lesson's truth:

> Stop poor sinner, stop and think
> Before you further go
> Will you sport upon the brink
> Of never ending woe?
> Once again I charge you stop
> For unless you warning take
> Ere you are aware you drop
> Into the burning lake.[22]

A third scheme for reaching children was the weeknight school at St. Peter's. The classes met in the evenings because most Dundee children worked, many in the city's factories, during the day. Over three hundred children enrolled in the school. The aim was to marry religion and learning. He told his workers, 'The chief use of the school is to convert the souls of the children.'[23]

---

21. Bonar, *MAR*, p. 513 (emphasis original).
22. MACCH 1.7.
23. Ibid. 3.3.38.

Parish visitation and the weekly ministries to children thrived. But he always longed for more. 'We may preach publicly, and from house to house; we may teach the young, and warn the old, but all will be in vain; *until* the Spirit be poured upon us from on high,' he affirmed.[24] The Spirit fell in 1839. The subsequent revival found him in his evangelistic element.

## Evangelism through Revival

The 'remarkable times' of revival in Scotland long fascinated M'Cheyne.[25] So he read their accounts and prayed earnestly to experience the Spirit's outpouring. He thought the Scotland of his day was unconcerned with Christ. Not long before he came to Dundee, he investigated the reasons for his country's spiritual slumber. He concluded: 'Perhaps, one reason we are not favoured with revival is, that we are not ready for it; the minister would not be able to direct people in their alarms.'[26]

M'Cheyne arrived at St. Peter's ever eager for revival. Longing for a shower of the Spirit was a main feature of the church's Thursday night prayer meetings. In 1837, he preached a well-regarded sermon from Jeremiah 14:8-9 that asked, 'Why is God a stranger in the Land?' The sermon gives M'Cheyne's perception of revival – what it is and how it comes. When revival comes to a nation, he explained, there are three noticeable consequences. First, 'There are always many awakened to a sense of sin and flocking to Christ.' Second, 'Not only are unconverted persons awakened and made to flee to Christ, but those who were in Christ before receive new measures of the Spirit.' Third, 'Open sinners, though they may remain unconverted, are often much restrained. There is an awe of God upon their spirits.'[27]

If those are the ordinary consequences of revival, what usually precedes the Spirit's arrival? M'Cheyne knew revival demands proper preaching. He pressed ministers to '*yearn over* men in the bowels of

---

24. M'Cheyne, *TBJ*, p. 117 (emphasis original).
25. MACCH 3.2.46.
26. Bonar, *Diary and Letters*, p. 27.
27. Ibid., *MAR*, p. 543.

Jesus Christ,' and to preach tenderly and persuasively.[28] Too many preachers, he believed, were content to scrape through their ministry by itching ears in the pulpits – not exalting Christ. 'We do not invite sinners tenderly, we do not gently woo them to Christ; we do not *compel* them to come in; we do not travail in birth till Christ be formed in them the hope of glory. Oh, who can wonder that God is such a stranger in the land?'[29]

Pastors were not the only group to fall under M'Cheyne's investigative eye. He also turned attention to the failings of church members. Their little interest in preaching and prayer was a damp cloth thrown on the means God's Spirit employs to ignite the church. He especially focused on the lack of prayer. No church that does not commit herself to private and public prayer should ever expect Christ's blessing, he warned. Additionally, the members' lack of personal holiness meant they had not been softened – and hard hearts will not encourage revival.

That revival came to Dundee while he was on the Mission of Inquiry to Palestine was no surprise to him. He had expressed hope that revival would come during his absence – maybe even *because* of his absence. He told Andrew Bonar:

> I sometimes think that a great blessing may come to my people in my absence. Often God does not bless us when we are in the midst of our labours, lest we shall say, 'My hand and my eloquence have done it.' He removes us into silence, and then pours 'down a blessing so that there is no room to receive it'; so that all that see it cry out, 'It is the Lord!' ... May it really be so with my dear people.[30]

The Dundee awakening generated strong opposition in some quarters of the Church. Some leaders postponed celebrating the Spirit's work until sufficient proof was provided. One such group was the Presbytery of Aberdeen. In December 1840, one year after the revival's start, the presbytery appointed a committee to research the recent revivals.

---

28. Ibid., p. 544.
29. Ibid., p. 544.
30. Ibid., p. 86. M'Cheyne's optimism for revival is seen as far back as 1837, when he announced that in his lifetime 'we shall have a time of reviving yet' (MACCH 3.1.6).

The committee sent M'Cheyne fifteen questions about the Dundee awakening. His answers were subsequently published as *Evidences on Revival*. If the 'Why is God a Stranger?' sermon gives his perception of revival, *Evidences* gives his experience of revival.

His response began with the revival's history in Dundee. He stated: 'A very remarkable and glorious work of God, in the conversion of sinners and edifying of saints, has taken place in this parish and neighborhood.'[31] He first emphasized the renewed hunger for God's Word. The awakening had begun when 'the word of God came with such power to the people here' that 'for nearly four months it was found desirable to have public worship almost every night.'[32] Further, a great spiritual gravity fell on the city: God's justice was frightening, Christ's sacrifice was sweet, holiness was prized, the Sabbath was sanctified, the worship was reverent, the prayers were earnest, the Sabbath Schools were overflowing, and private meetings for prayer abounded. M'Cheyne reported: 'The change they have undergone might be enough to convince an atheist that there is a God, or an infidel that there is a Saviour.'[33]

What's especially notable in the Dundee revival is how it vindicated his conviction that awakening comes through holy preaching and prayer. M'Cheyne indeed believed the Spirit is sovereign in times of revival. He wrote:

> [The Holy Spirit] comes like the pouring rain; sometimes like the gentle dew. Still I would humbly state my conviction, that it is the duty of all who seek the salvation of souls, and especially the duty of ministers, to long and pray for such solemn times, when the arrows shall be sharp in the heart of the King's enemies and our slumbering congregations shall be made to cry out, 'Men and brethren, what shall we do?'[34]

The Spirit's sovereignty does not erase the means He uses to awaken God's people. The new vibrancy found in Burns' and M'Cheyne's preaching was how they sought 'the *immediate* conversion of the people'

---

31. Ibid., p. 497.
32. Ibid., p. 497.
33. Ibid., p. 498.
34. Ibid., p. 501.

and believed that 'under a living gospel ministry, success is more or less the rule, and want of success is the exception.'[35]

M'Cheyne emphasized prayer even more than preaching in his pursuit of revival. Not only was prayer of pivotal importance to the start of the awakening, but it was clear evidence of revival. Prayer calls upon the Holy Spirit to descend in power and to continue to do so. He believed that anointed revival preachers are 'peculiarly given to secret prayer; and they have also been accustomed to have much united prayer when together, and especially before and after engaging in public worship.'[36] Local churches played a key role as well: 'If we go on in faith and prayer … God will hear the cry of His people and … we shall yet see days such as never before shone upon the Church of Scotland.'[37]

## Evangelism through Church Extension

The final component in M'Cheyne's evangelistic program was his work for church extension – what we more commonly call 'church planting' today.

In 1837, M'Cheyne became the secretary of the Committee for Church Extension in Forfarshire. He wrote to a fellow pastor:

> Every day I live, I feel more and more persuaded that [church extension] is the cause of God and of his kingdom in Scotland in our day. Many a time, when I thought myself a dying man, the souls of the perishing thousands in my own parish, who never enter any house of God, have lain heavy on my heart. Many a time have I prayed that the eyes of our enemies might be opened, and that God would open the hearts of our rulers, to feel that their highest duty and greatest glory is to support the ministers of Christ, and to send these to every perishing soul in Scotland.[38]

M'Cheyne eventually became the secretary of the Dundee Association for Church Extension. His campaign for new churches created nearly two hundred churches and an enormous collection of more than £300,000 over seven years.[39] For M'Cheyne, God pours out His Spirit

---

35. Ibid., p. 503 (emphasis original).
36. Ibid., p. 503.
37. M'Cheyne, *TPH*, p. 166.
38. Quoted in Bonar, *MAR*, pp. 69-70.
39. Such a sum would be roughly equivalent to £38 million or $49 million in 2019.

on churches. Therefore, more faithful churches means more buckets to collect the Spirit's rain. He even wrote a short poem to express his zeal for church extension:

> Give me a man of God the truth to preach,
> A house of prayer within convenient reach,
> Seat-rents the poorest of the poor can pay,
> A spot so small one pastor can survey,
> Give these – and give the Spirit's genial shower,
> Scotland shall be a garden all in flower![40]

## Conclusion

M'Cheyne's wide-ranging zeal for evangelism challenges our small attempts today. His gospel labor rested on a few simple convictions. The first was love for Christ. The reason why he could wake each morning looking to share Christ is because his communion with Jesus was constant. Fellowship with Christ increases love for Him. And souls that love Christ are lives that speak of Him. A heart burning with love to Jesus will inevitably share the good news of Christ.

Additionally, M'Cheyne's devotion to prayer infused every part of his ministry. A ministry that does not ask, will not have. He prayed constantly for conversion. He longed for it. He asked for it. He expected it. And he received it.

Finally, and this cannot be missed, M'Cheyne worked hard. He had a native gifting for evangelism. But he nonetheless exercised it with tireless fervor. He asked St. Peter's, 'Who will forsake father and mother, houses and land, to carry the message of a Saviour to these [sinners]?'[41] He told of the Moravian missionaries 'impelled by a divine love for souls' who chose such a field for harvest. He saw in these missionaries a paradigm for biblical evangelism: 'Ah! my dear friends, may we [be like] these men in vehement, heart-consuming love to Jesus and the souls of men.'[42]

---

40. Bonar, *MAR*, p. 70.
41. Ibid., p. 200.
42. Ibid., p. 200.

# CHAPTER 8

# M'Cheyne and Resting in Christ

THE legend of M'Cheyne's personal piety tends to overshadow a key truth in his pastoral program: he was keenly interested – and active – in ecclesiastical affairs. He knew the broader movements affecting the Church of Scotland. He led St. Peter's to pray for various matters facing the Kirk. As a devoted member of the evangelical party, he labored and lobbied for its long-term aims.

Few topics better show his ecclesiastical labor as does his work for entire obedience to the Fourth Commandment: 'You shall keep the Sabbath holy.' Through what would become known as the Sabbath Railway Controversy, his zeal for Christ stood out with unique force. In the controversy, we see how public polemics were not at all beyond him. Such polemical fervor adds a fresh texture to the portrait of piety frequently attached to him. His work to see the whole Lord's Day sanctified earned him monikers such as the 'wild man from Dundee,' 'fanatic' and 'zealot,' and the man full of 'invective.'[1] One Scottish minister complained that Andrew Bonar's Sabbath-keeping zeal was 'bad enough, but [M'Cheyne's] is ten times waur!'[2]

M'Cheyne's passion for keeping the Sabbath can strike many today as too intense – even legalistic. What is wrong with mail trains running on Sunday? Why should his arguments be so abrasive?

---

1. Marjorie Bonar, *Reminiscences*, p. 9. 'Scotsman,' 9 April 1842; Yeaworth, p. 325.
2. Ibid., p. 9.

As with virtually everything in his life, love for Christ motivated his action. He believed Sunday was *the Lord's Day*; the entire day should thus belong to the Savior. 'The Sabbath is Christ's trysting time with His church,' he preached. 'If you love Him, you will count every moment of it precious. You will rise early and sit up late, to have a long day with Christ.'[3] Little love for the Lord's Day reveals little love for Christ. But when the heart longs for communion with Jesus, there will always be a growing sanctification of the Lord's Day.

M'Cheyne also emphasized Lord's Day devotion because it was an integral part of pastoral piety. He asked, 'Can you name one godly minister, of any denomination in all Scotland, who does not hold the duty of the entire sanctification of the Lord's day?'[4] Godliness means obedience to God's law. M'Cheyne, like virtually every pastor of his time, understood the Ten Commandments as 'the moral law.' Whereas other Old Testament ceremonial and civil laws passed away through Christ's finished work, the moral law remains binding. Any true holiness will thus demonstrate a delight in the Fourth Commandment. Jesus commented, 'If you love me, you will keep my commandments' (John 14:15). M'Cheyne simply asked, 'Should we not show love to the Lord through our Sabbath-keeping?'

To understand M'Cheyne's passionate polemics related to Sabbath-keeping, we must first see the context surrounding the Sabbath Railroad Controversy. For it was in this context that his hottest pleas for obedience to the Fourth Commandment came.

## The Sabbath Railroad Controversy

The ordeal stretched back to the early 1830s, but truly got going in 1839. That year a group of passionate evangelicals formed the 'Society for Promoting the Due Observance of the Lord's Day.' The Society's initial purpose was to combat the planned expansion of rail traffic on Sundays. Chairman Andrew Agnew thundered against 'the threatened invasion of Sabbath-breaking customs from England by the railways.'[5]

---

3. M'Cheyne, *TPP*, p. 330.
4. Bonar, *MAR*, p. 553.
5. T. McCrie, quoted in C. J. A. Robertson, p. 145.

Although trains had run on Sundays for some time in England, the practice had yet to cross into Scotland. The Scottish people were used to the rails stopping completely on the Lord's Day. Scottish evangelicals reveled in their devotion to the Sabbath. They were, after all, a country covenanted to Christ.

Yet, in the late 1830s major rail companies began to think about opening the rails on Sunday. In 1841, the Edinburgh & Glasgow Company proposed instituting two Sunday trains running in each direction the following year. The proposal was called 'a great and startling *innovation*.'[6] Subsequent outcry from Kirk Sessions and Sabbatarian partisans caused the company to postpone a final decision on opening the rails until early 1842.

## M'Cheyne's Labor During the Controversy

It was in 1841 that M'Cheyne entered the debate. And he entered with a flurry of activity. First, he convened the 'Sabbath Observance Committee' in his presbytery. In February 1841, the presbytery appointed him to write a letter to the Dundee & Arbroath rail company, which was evaluating mail delivery by rail on Sundays. His broadside against such action was worded so strongly that it needed revision before publication. The next month saw him penning an overture to that year's General Assembly. The overture's message was simple: excommunicate unrepentant Sabbath breakers.

By the end of 1841, M'Cheyne was ready to take on what he saw as the major offender in the controversy – the Edinburgh & Glasgow Company. On 1 December, he posted a letter to Alexander M'Neill, director of the rail giant. A conservative periodical, *The Witness*, published the letter ten days later. His polemics were now available for all to see. And his polemics packed a punch.

M'Cheyne opened the letter by saying, 'I take leave to express in this manner the deep feelings of righteous indignation.'[7] He was careful, at least initially, to not impugn unnecessarily the director's plan. He

---

6. C. J. A. Robertson, p. 153 (emphasis original).
7. Bonar, *MAR*, p. 555. All subsequent quotes from the letter are taken from *MAR*, pp. 555-57.

wondered, however, if M'Neill was not fully forthright with the public. 'Ah! sir, speak out your mind,' he urged the director, 'Tell what it is that lies at the bottom of your enmity to the entire preservation of the Lord's day.' M'Neill's initial press release stated his company's need to submit to God's law, so M'Cheyne could not fathom how such a statement squared with the proposed rail plan. 'I do not know whether the motion has come entirely from your own mind, or whether several have agreed with you in it; but I here freely state my convictions, formed upon the calm and deliberate study of the motion, and without the slightest desire to use a harsh or improper term, that THE MOTION IS BLASPHEMOUS,' he announced. The remainder of the letter proceeds with the young pastor's standard defense of Sabbath-keeping. By the end, he was ready to adjudicate the matter. He told M'Neill: 'You prove, even to the blind world, that you are not journeying toward the Sabbath above, where the Sabbath-breaker cannot come.'

Appended to M'Cheyne's letter was a postscript appealing to the law of 1690 that mandated strict observance of the Sabbath. The short P.S. is significant when trying to comprehend his supposed vehemence. He belonged to a lineage of Presbyterian ministers who viewed Scotland as a covenanted country. He was content to call Scotland 'the likest of all lands to ancient Israel.' 'Scotland may be called God's second Israel,' he declared. 'No other land has its Sabbath as Scotland has.'[8] These convictions are partly why he was so shocked to discover, while on the Mission of Inquiry, how little Sabbath-keeping could be found outside of Scotland. In early December of 1841, he announced to St. Peter's: 'If the day shall ever come in Scotland when our railways shall be opened on the Sabbath, it will be one of the finishing marks that the people of this land are not the people of God.'[9]

M'Cheyne's public advance against the rail companies increased throughout December 1841. He preached numerous sermons calling for Sabbath-keeping. On 18 December, *The Witness* published his tract, *I Love the Lord's Day*. The booklet is – on the whole – winsome and warm. Yet as in the case with his letter to M'Neill, it is ultimately a fighting document. His verdict on Sabbath-breakers is resolute: they

---

8. Ibid., p. 449.
9. M'Cheyne, *BOH*, p. 33.

are infidels, scoffers, men of unholy lives, enemies of all righteousness, moral suicides, sinners against light, traitors to their country, robbers, and murderers.[10] His sermon, 'The Stone the Builders Refused,' on which *I Love the Lord's Day* was based, concluded with a blast: 'Dear brethren, pray that their hearts may be turned or else if that may not be, that the Railway may be swept off the face of the earth.'[11]

The Edinburgh & Glasgow Railroad Company shareholders met in February 1842 to decide the matter. Two days before, M'Cheyne published yet another letter in *The Witness* calling for a national day of prayer. He asked for united prayer 'THAT THE DESIGNS OF THE RAILWAY SABBATH-BREAKERS MAY BE ENTIRELY DEFEATED.'[12] He urged Christians to rise two hours early to fast and to confess personal, family, and national sin. He also asked ministers to intercede for the conversion of Sabbath-breakers.

M'Cheyne's efforts and prayers went unheeded. The shareholders decided to run the Sunday trains. The evangelical leaders would not go quietly, however. For three months William Chalmers Burns, M'Cheyne's great friend, preached every Lord's Day at the Haymarket Station in Edinburgh, heralding Christ as Lord of the Sabbath. Letters and literature arguing for renewed Sabbath-keeping continued to pour forth in periodicals. By 1845, the trains were stopped on Sunday. They would not open for another twenty years.

How then should we understand M'Cheyne's role in the controversy? Was he too strong and overzealous? Or were his polemics indeed full of sincere love for Christ? We can only answer such questions after seeing, in more detail, why and how M'Cheyne strove for keeping the entire Sabbath holy to Christ.

## M'Cheyne's Defense of Sabbath-Keeping

M'Cheyne was no doctrinal innovator. The Westminster Confession of Faith was his theology in summary form. The Confession's chapter on the Sabbath is chapter twenty-one, 'Of Religious Worship, and the

---

10. Bonar, *MAR*, p. 553.
11. M'Cheyne, *TPP*, p. 31.
12. M'Cheyne, 'To the Children of God of Every Name in Scotland,' in *The Witness*, 19 February 1842 (capitalization original).

Sabbath Day.' The document asserts: 'This Sabbath is then kept holy unto the Lord, when men, after a due preparing of their hearts, and ordering of their common affairs beforehand, do not only observe an holy rest, all the day, from their own works, words, and thoughts about their worldly employments and recreations, but also are taken up, the whole time, in the public and private exercises of his worship, and in the duties of necessity and mercy.'[13]

M'Cheyne's stance towards the Sabbath was typical for the evangelical party in the Church. He understood obedience to the Fourth Commandment as unquestionable. Therefore, much of his Sabbath material does not provide an in-depth defense of the Sabbatarian position. A brief sketch of his comments on the Lord's Day show that he consistently emphasized six truths to promote obedience on the Sabbath.

First, the Lord's Day mirrors God's pattern in creation. When God rested on the seventh day (Gen. 2:2-3), He did so not out of need. He rested for our sake 'that He might set an example to man.'[14]

Second, observing the Lord's Day is a clear command. M'Cheyne explained: 'When God took Israel to be a peculiar people to Himself, He revived, in a very clear and terrible manner, the holy law which was written on man's heart in the day of his creation.'[15] By twice writing the Ten Commandments with His own finger on the stone tablets, God demonstrated that they are perpetual. Just as the other nine commandments are valid in the New Covenant age, so is the fourth.

Third, the Lord's Day has a typological function. M'Cheyne believed the Sabbath is a type of heaven on earth. Devotion to the Lord's Day connects a believer with the life to come:

> When a believer lays aside his pen or loom, brushes aside his worldly cares, leaving them behind him with his week-day clothes, and comes up to the house of God, it is like the morning of the resurrection, the day when we shall come out of great tribulation into the presence of God and the Lamb. When he sits under the preached word, and hears the voice of the shepherd leading and feeding his soul, it reminds him of the day when the Lamb that

---

13. *WCF* 21.8.
14. M'Cheyne, *NTS*, p. 37.
15. Ibid., p. 38.

is in the midst of the throne shall feed him and lead him to living fountains of waters. When he joins in the psalm of praise, it reminds him of the day when his hands shall strike the harp of God. When he retires, and meets with God in secret in his closet, or, like Isaac, in some favourite spot near his dwelling, it reminds him of the day when 'he shall be a pillar in the house of our God, and go no more out' (Rev. 3:12).[16]

Fourth, the Lord's Day is a day of evangelism. M'Cheyne believed that God especially exercises His power on Sundays. The Sabbath is thus a day uniquely suited for converting sinners. His logic was biblical and simple. Because the church gathers on Sundays for preaching, prayer, fellowship, and the sacraments, she should believe an extraordinary power will be present. It is through these means that God breathes life into dead bones. M'Cheyne maintained: 'There is nothing superstitious in believing that we may expect more visits of Christ and of the Spirit on the Lord's Day than on other days.'[17] The Sabbath, then, is Christ's market-day for souls.

Fifth, the Lord's Day is a time of blessing. The Father hallowed the Sabbath when He rested on it. Likewise, Christ blessed Sunday by rising from the grave on it. Throughout the gospels we find Jesus blessing His people on Sunday (e.g., John 10:19; 20:26). The Spirit blessed the Lord's Day by falling on the church in power on Sunday. M'Cheyne thus concluded: 'So that in all ages, from the beginning of the world, and in every place where there is a believer, the Sabbath has been a day of double blessing. It is so still.'[18]

Sixth, observing the Lord's Day is historic Christian practice. M'Cheyne's conviction that Sunday is the Christian Sabbath was the assumed position in Scotland during his pastorate. His exposition of Acts 20:6-7 took it for granted that the Sabbath changed from Saturday to Sunday. He proclaimed, 'Here Paul waited over the Jewish Sabbath and preached and broke bread on the Lord's Day. Upon the same day did Paul command religious contributions to be made (1 Cor 15:1-2).'[19] So important was the historicity of Lord's Day devotion that M'Cheyne did

---

16. Bonar, *MAR*, p. 549.
17. M'Cheyne, *TPP*, p. 331.
18. Bonar, *MAR*, p. 551.
19. M'Cheyne, *TPP*, p. 329.

something unusual in his preaching: he called on secondary sources. When he spoke about the historicity of Sabbath-keeping, he often read from Justin Martyr's *Apology for Christians*, which explained, 'All the Christians that live either in the town or country meet together at the same place upon the day called Sunday, where the writings of the prophets and apostles are read.'[20]

M'Cheyne's sermons on Sabbath-keeping engage with standard objections. He answered questions such as, 'Does not Sabbath observance belong to the Old Covenant order of Judaism?' 'What about Matthew 5:17 – does not Jesus "fulfill" the law?' 'Should not every day be a Sabbath to the Lord?' 'What evidence is there really for the day changing from Saturday to Sunday?'

All in all, there is no novelty in M'Cheyne's defense of Sabbath-observance. His position was that of his Puritan and evangelical Presbyterian predecessors.

## M'Cheyne's Personal Pattern of Sabbath-Keeping

Many of M'Cheyne's most famous quotes come from diary entries that were made on the Lord's Day. In fact, of the one hundred and sixty-three dated entries in M'Cheyne's diary, eighteen were written on a Monday, nineteen on a Tuesday, seventeen on a Wednesday, twenty-one on a Thursday, eleven on a Friday, sixteen on a Saturday, and sixty on a Sunday. Our view of his spirituality thus depends, to a great extent, on how he spent his Sabbaths – in public and in private.

For example, one oft-quoted statement from M'Cheyne's diary is, 'Rose early to seek God, and found Him whom my soul loveth. Who would not rise early to meet such company?'[21] Many used the quote to exhort Christians to redeem the earliest hours for Christ. The plea is true in its basic form. However, when we recognize that he wrote it on the Lord's Day, we see that his earliest rising was always on the Lord's Day. He believed that Christ promised special communion on Sunday. In light of such a promise, he asked, who would not want to spend as much time with the Lord?

---

20. Ibid., p. 329.
21. Bonar, *MAR*, p. 21.

The Sabbath was the day of M'Cheyne's sweetest communion with Christ. It was when he most movingly poured out his soul. Andrew Bonar remembered that keeping the Sabbath holy was a first fruit of his friend's conversion. 'Mr. M'Cheyne's own conduct was in full accordance with his principles in regard to strict yet cheerful Sabbath observance,' Bonar recalled. 'Considering it the summit of human privilege to be admitted to fellowship with God, his principle was, that the Lord's Day was to be spent wholly in the enjoyment of that sweetest privilege.'[22]

M'Cheyne's Sabbath pattern was clear and consistent. He aimed to go to bed early on Saturday so he could rise early on Sunday. He often set Saturday evening aside for prayer and fasting to prepare his heart for the Lord's Day. He also made a point to visit the dying on Saturdays 'with the view of being thus stirred up to a more direct application of the truth to his flock on the morrow, as dying men on the edge of eternity.'[23] After waking on Sunday, M'Cheyne tried to spend a few hours in private prayer. Then he read God's Word. On Sundays, he also examined any notes from the previous week's devotional readings, meditating on any verse marked for special attention. He did not work on his sermons, believing that the Lord's Day was for 'the refreshment of his soul.'[24] Outside of preaching and devotional hours, he spent the Sabbath visiting, evangelizing, and conversing about Christ. He spent particular time confessing his sins. 'I ought, on Sabbath evenings,' he wrote, 'to be especially careful to confess the sins of holy things.'[25] The emphasis on confessing sin stemmed from his conviction that 'all sin is double sin on the Sabbath. It is a day of double blessing and double cursing.'[26]

## M'Cheyne's Congregational Exhortation to Sabbath-Keeping

Many Christians, when thinking about Sabbath observance, often ask, 'What am I not allowed to do on the Lord's Day?' M'Cheyne focused his shepherding about Sabbath spirituality away from the day's duty to the

---

22. Ibid., p. 141.
23. Ibid., p. 76.
24. Ibid., p. 56.
25. Ibid., p. 152.
26. From his class notes on the Catechism quoted in Yeaworth, pp. 322-23.

day's delight. He regularly declared, 'How sweet is the Sabbath morning!' With the prophet Isaiah, he longed for his church to 'call the Sabbath a delight' (Isa. 58:13). He gave many exhortations to St. Peter's about keeping the Lord's Day. In particular, four stand out most prominent.

First, he taught how keeping the Lord's Day is a matter of sincerity. 'I do not ask if you love the *externals* of the Sabbath day, the exciting sermon, the meeting with friends, the singing of praises,' he commented. 'But do you love the *internals* of a holy Sabbath? The communion with God; the delighting in Him; loving, adoring, admiring Him.'[27] He knew Satan tempts professing Christians to mere outward obedience. Formalists may keep their foot from slipping on the Sabbath, but they still profane the day internally. What God wants is sincere obedience, a heart-felt love for Christ that delights to devote the day to Him.

Second, the Lord's Day is a proper time for examination. 'There cannot be a better test of whether you are saved or lost than whether you delight in the Sabbath,' he announced.[28] Ever the evangelist, he believed that Sabbath-observance revealed one's love for Christ. His typical exhortations on this point include,

> 'The Sabbath is Christ's trysting time with His church. If you love Him, you will count every moment of it precious.'

> 'Did you ever meet with a child of God, one who bore the image of Christ, who did not love to spend a holy Sabbath day?'

> 'Everyone that has a new heart regards the Sabbath as holy ground.'

> 'If anyone has come to Christ, he will not make it either a day of merchandise or a day of pleasure excursions.'

> 'Only believers spend the Sabbath in exalting Christ in their own hearts, getting their hearts more and more rooted and built up in Him.'

> 'Have you a peculiar taste for the Sabbath day? Do you love a well-spent Sabbath? If so, you have one mark that you are passed from death to life.'[29]

---

27. M'Cheyne, *NTS*, p. 41 (emphasis original).
28. Ibid., *SOH*, p. 33.
29. Ibid., *TPP*, p. 332; M'Cheyne, *NTS*, p. 39; M'Cheyne, *OTS*, pp. 91, 95 M'Cheyne, *NTS*, pp. 39, 40.

Third, the Lord's Day is a day ripe for repentance. If one does not love the Sabbath here on earth, why would you love an eternal Sabbath in heaven? He thus used a laxity towards the Lord's Day as a simple opportunity to urge unbelievers to repent and turn to Christ.

Fourth, the Lord's Day fuels growth in holiness. Christ is the model of true piety, and thus the epitome of faithful Sabbath-keeping. M'Cheyne reminded his church that Jesus 'loved the holy Sabbath.'[30] Sabbath-days 'are like milestones' guiding us along the way to holiness.[31]

The Lord's Day brings rest for weary souls and food for hungry hearts. For those who wanted to know how to observe the Sabbath, M'Cheyne encouraged them to consider the saints' work in heaven. The chief joy of heaven is meeting with God; thus, we ought to spend our Sabbaths in God's presence. And just as beholding Christ is the apex of heaven, so too should looking on the Lord be the continual delight of the Sabbath.

## Conclusion

Some (maybe most?) Christians today will find M'Cheyne's Sabbath convictions too ardent. Sincere, yes; but overblown. If we are humble and open to a different view, his delight in the Sabbath should challenge the apathy – even antipathy – toward keeping the Lord's Day.

M'Cheyne's convictions confront our love for Christ. We will never understand his labor for 'keeping the entire Lord's Day' if we do not see how he believed Sunday was *the Lord's* Day. The day belongs to Christ. 'We love everything that is Christ's,' he stated. 'We love the *Lord's day*, because it is His.'[32] This is why M'Cheyne thought one's approach to the Sabbath was such a clear indicator of whether or not that person belonged to the Lord. 'Do you love the Lord? You will then certainly love to keep His day holy,' he would say.

Connecting M'Cheyne's love for Christ to his passion for the Lord's Day helps make sense of his public polemics. He saw the Church and the nation's love for the Sabbath waning. In his mind, that could only

---

30. Ibid., *TPH*, p. 357.
31. Bonar, *MAR*, p. 343.
32. Ibid., p. 548 (emphasis original).

lead to one conclusion: love for Christ was on the decline. What godly pastor would not raise the alarm at such a prospect?

The Sabbath-Railroad ordeal also allows us to see how M'Cheyne's maturity was a *public* piety. His private devotion always had a *telos* in the public exaltation of Christ. A true pursuit of Jesus is necessarily a public reality. The Spirit means that the sanctification of God's people should function as a magnet, drawing the world to look on Christ in love.

Earnest simplicity. Holy sincerity. These are phrases that define M'Cheyne's love for Christ. And few places vindicate their truth as does his devotion to the Lord's Day.

# CHAPTER 9

# M'Cheyne and Looking for Christ

IN the main, Robert Murray M'Cheyne was a typical evangelical Presbyterian when it came to his theology. There is, however, one doctrinal element that stands out as peculiar for his time: his eschatology. His eschatology was so irregular in his day that it earned him and other adherents the label 'the Evangelical Light Infantry.'[1]

Theologically speaking, M'Cheyne is usually called a 'millenarian.' Yet, as we shall soon see, he is better understood as a 'hesitant millenarian.' Part of the difficulty in categorizing his view of the last things is that contemporary categories of premillennial, amillennial, and postmillennial (and not to mention the various refinements of those groups!) cannot express adequately the exegesis of his time. His day did not have the level of eschatological precisionism as we have today. Only two eschatological categories were common during his ministry. There were (1) 'millennialists,' people who were optimists and gradualists when thinking about the future, and (2) 'millenarians,' those who were more pessimistic and radical. The vast majority of Scottish ministers and Christians living in the early-to-mid nineteenth century were firm millennialists. They believed culture was growing in a Godward direction. The future was bright. Reasons for worldwide hope abounded.

---

1. Murray, p. 217. Light Infantry soldiers were used as a skirmishing screen. They were smaller in number and deployed to slow down the advancing enemy, ahead of the main infantry's advance.

Comprehending M'Cheyne's eschatological ethic begins with asking a simple question, 'Who influenced his eschatology?'

## Influences on M'Cheyne's Eschatology

M'Cheyne was a capable exegete. He was adept in the original languages of God's Word and aware of interpretive history. But he did not arrive at his eschatological views in a vacuum. The two ministers who most shaped his mind on millenarianism were Edward Irving and Andrew Bonar. The first was nothing less than a celebrity in Scotland – although one who eventually fell from the Church of Scotland's graces. The second was a close friend, whose apologetics for millenarianism were more pronounced than many remember.

### The Influence of Edward Irving

Edward Irving (1792–1834) was something of a King Saul in his day. He was tall and handsome. He commanded the attention of the masses. Everything about him oozed appeal. His ministerial career began as an assistant to Thomas Chalmers. In 1821, he accepted a call to pastor the Caledonian Church in London. Massive crowds thronged to hear his captivating rhetoric. People from the highest places of society filled the pews – artists, philosophers, politicians, and aristocrats. Over the next decade, his theology became more innovative and problematic. He began to teach the doctrine of 'Christ's sinful flesh,' which held that His humanity was identical with mankind's, meaning he had sinful, fleshly propensities. Irving's error was egregious enough for the Church to depose him in 1833 for heresy. He died the next year, leaving his fledging Catholic Apostolic Church to pave the way for twentieth century Pentecostalism. Christology and pneumatology aside, it is in the area of eschatology that Irving should be understood.

Irving caused no small stir in the mid 1820s with his millenarian teaching. He had discovered the millenarian work of Manuel Lacunza, a South American Jesuit. Irving published Lacunza's work under the title, *The Coming of the Messiah in Glory and Majesty.* A main feature in Lacunza's teaching, one that Irving promoted, was a literalist view of interpretation. Ironically, the Roman Catholic Church was so concerned with Lacuna's hermeneutic that his book was banned by the authorities, yet it was a primary force in shaping premillennial thinking in Britain.

Irving sat at the feet of Lacunza and other radical millenarians, absorbing their views. By the late 1820s, he found two main outlets to publicize his increasingly radical eschatology: The Albury Conference and the *Morning Watch* (or *Quarterly Journal of Prophecy*). The first was an influential annual prophecy conference in which Irving participated from 1826 to 1830. The second was a significant periodical that broadcasted his view to the English-speaking world.

What did Irving teach? The central elements were:

That the 'Christian dispensation' will not pass gradually into the millennial state (contra the dominant millennialist position). It will happen as suddenly as the Temple was destroyed in A.D. 70.

When the final judgments come on Christendom, the Jews will be restored to their land.

The final judgments will begin with Christendom.

The end of these judgments will usher in Christ's millennial reign on earth.

Christ's second coming precedes the millennium.

The Lord's appearance is coming soon.

One scholar concludes: 'Irving's belief in the literal and imminent personal return of Christ was the most distinctive aspect of his appeal and a significant innovation in Evangelical doctrine. While the prophetic texts of the Bible had been extensively studied during the eighteenth century, this scholarship was not essentially millenarian.... Little attention was devoted to the unfulfilled prophecies of the Bible or to the second coming of the Messiah.'[2]

In the centuries since M'Cheyne died, many have noticed similarities between M'Cheyne's millenarianism and that of Edward Irving. What influence did Irving have on him? Nothing direct. He read some of Irving's writings and logged a list of 'Rules for Interpreting Symbolical Prophecy.'[3] Also, in a diary entry on 9 November 1834, he mentioned

2. Ralph Brown, p. 679.
3. See MACCH 1.3, pp. 9-15.

Irving's death: 'Heard of Edward Irving's death. I look back upon him with awe, as on the saints and martyrs of old. A holy man in spite of all his delusions and errors. He is now with his God and Saviour, whom he wronged so much, yet, I am persuaded, loved so sincerely.'[4] We have no record of him ever meeting Irving face to face. M'Cheyne never attended The Albury Conference.

But Andrew Bonar attended Irving's teaching. And Bonar was as ardent a millenarian as could be found in the Church of Scotland.

## The Influence of Andrew Bonar

In 1828, before he was converted, Bonar listened spellbound to Irving's lectures on prophecy. The next year, he wrote in a diary entry: 'Have been hearing Mr. Irving's lectures all the week, and am persuaded now that his views of the Coming of Christ are truth. The views of the glory of Christ opened up in his lectures have been very impressive to me.'[5] Not long after his conversion, Bonar spoke about his grief over how many opposed Christ's coming before the millennium. When he arrived at the Divinity Hall in 1831, he found a perfect outlet to disseminate his eschatology in Chalmers' Exegetical Society. George Smith, the biographer of Alexander Somerville (M'Cheyne's good friend and member of the Exegetical Society), gives insight into Bonar's millenarian enthusiasm:

> Millenarian theories were discussed, *chiefly under Andrew Bonar's influence*. McCheyne looked with interest on these, but did not commit himself to adopting them fully. Somerville denounced such speculation as 'dangerous,' but always with shrewd humour. ... The point was referred to [Chalmers], who took McCheyne's position. He had not so fully studied these views as his young friends, but saw no danger in holding them.[6]

The friendship between M'Cheyne and Bonar brought long discussions on the millennium. There is noticeable affinity between the two regarding Christ's sudden appearance before His thousand-year reign. What is also noticeable is how M'Cheyne's eschatology lacks the bite that Bonar's

---

4. Bonar, *MAR*, p. 25.
5. Ibid., *Diary and Life*, p. 5.
6. Smith, p. 18 (emphasis added).

did. In 1837, Bonar wrote in his diary that he was feeling 'cast down' because he had been 'kept out of several appointments' because of his 'millenarianism chiefly.'[7] When the Mission of Inquiry was appointed, Bonar's millenarian zeal was divisive enough that many did not want to send him. The officers, in time, relented. After M'Cheyne's death, St. Peter's refused to extend a call to Bonar because, by his own account, 'many of the electors could not bear my views of Christ's advent.'[8]

Andrew Bonar was the real shaping influence on M'Cheyne's eschatology. M'Cheyne looked appreciatively on Irving's scheme. He indeed agreed with much of Bonar's system – which would now be called historic premillennialism. Yet, his view was ultimately quite hesitant. Bonar recalled how

> At a time when he was apparently in his usual health, we were talking together on the subject of the Premillennial Advent. We had begun to speak of the practical influence which the belief of that doctrine might have. At length he said, 'that he saw no force in the arguments generally urged against it, though he had difficulties of his own in regard to it. And perhaps (he added), it is well for you… to be so firmly persuaded that Christ is thus to come.'[9]

## M'Cheyne's Eschatology-Shaped Spirituality

A careful study of M'Cheyne's preaching shows that, much like his position on the Sabbath, he took the premillennial return of Christ as something of a given. He never used the world 'millennium' in any published sermon. He never referenced a thousand-year reign of Christ that immediately followed the Lord's return.

M'Cheyne was less concerned with the order of eschatology than he was with the Christ of eschatology. His eschatology was not for debating or defending. It was for evangelism. It was for growth in Christ. His whole eschatological scheme can be summarized in the following lines from a sermon on Mark 13:34-37:

> I am far from discouraging those who seek to enquire from prophecy when the coming of the Saviour shall be – it is a most interesting enquiry – and

---

7. Bonar, *Diary and Letters*, p. 57.
8. Ibid., p. 105.
9. Ibid., *MAR*, p. 84.

it shows us little caring about the Saviour if we care little about the time. Neither am I an enemy to those who argue from what they see in the church and the world that the time is at hand.... But what we are taught is... (1) Christ shall come; (2) He shall come suddenly.[10]

A proper response to Christ's immanent return meant a few things for M'Cheyne. First, he emphasized missionary endeavors to the Jews. He believed in a 'final conversion' of Israel,[11] a world-changing event 'yet to come.'[12] He emphasized how God will 'awaken the Jews in the latter day'[13] and that Israel will be 'restored' to their ancient land.[14] Such convictions bridged whatever partisan aisle in the Church of Scotland's collective eschatology. Moderate and evangelicals alike agreed in the future hope for Israel. At the 1838 General Assembly, no less than sixteen overtures were put forth related to the Jews, calling the Church to evangelize God's ancient people.

M'Cheyne's belief in the future conversion of Israel fueled in him a longing for revival. He told his parents:

> To seek the lost sheep of the house of Israel is an object very near to my heart, as my people know it has ever been. Such an enterprise may probably draw down unspeakable blessings on the Church of Scotland, according to the promise, 'they shall prosper who love thee'.... I feel convinced that if we pray that the world may be converted in God's way, we will seek the Good of the Jews, and the more we do so, the happier we will be in our own souls. You should always keep up a knowledge of the prophecies regarding Israel.[15]

M'Cheyne expected a shower of the Spirit to fall on any church aiming to reach the Jews for Christ. That revival came to Dundee while he was on mission to Israel only solidified this conviction. He plainly believed God still had a peculiar love for Israel. To walk worthy of the Lord meant pursuing the Jewish people for Jesus. He exhorted Christians to 'be like God in his peculiar affections; and the whole Bible shows

---

10. M'Cheyne, *NTS*, pp. 42-43.
11. Ibid., *TPH*, p. 429.
12. Ibid., p. 224.
13. Ibid., p. 439.
14. Ibid., *OTS*, p. 156.
15. Bonar, *MAR*, p. 88.

that God has ever had, and still has, a peculiar love to the Jews.'[16] For M'Cheyne, the Jews' conversion to Christ would not just give life to dead and dying churches, it would also hasten the return of Jesus.

To this Israel-centric missionary impulse, M'Cheyne wed urgency to his evangelism. From the start of his ministry, it is clear that he did not expect to live long. Maybe it was a premonition from the Spirit. Or maybe he knew his poor health would lead to an early reckoning. Whatever it was, his view of life's brevity catalyzed his already earnest evangelism.

Not that he thought himself faithful in this regard. He chided himself when saying, 'Time is short, my time especially, and souls are precious; and I fear many are slumbering because I watch not with sufficient diligence, nor blow the trumpet with sufficient clearness.'[17] Preachers who know the reality of eternity are those who speak most plainly. They know souls hang on eternity's precipice in each sermon. Judgment might fall at any moment. Thus, he cried, 'Oh, believers, it is the duty of ministers to preach with [Judgment Day] in their eye! … Would not this take away fear of man? Would not this make us urgent in our preaching? You must either get these souls into Christ, or you will yet see them lying down in everlasting burnings.'[18]

Not only should eternity's reality compel urgent preaching, M'Cheyne believed it ought to infuse all Lord's Day services with earnestness and expectancy. He told a ministerial friend:

> May your mind be solemnized, my dear friend, by the thought that we are ministers but for a time; that the Master may summon us to retire into silence, or may call us to the temple above; or the midnight cry of the great Bridegroom may break suddenly on our ears. Blessed is the servant that is found waiting! Make all your services tell for eternity; speak what you can look back upon with comfort when you must be silent.[19]

---

16. Ibid., p. 88.
17. Ibid., p. 244.
18. Ibid., p. 359. See also M'Cheyne, *BOF*, pp. 90-91, 130, 140, 154-55, 161, 163, 169; M'Cheyne, *HTD*, p. 77; M'Cheyne, *NTS*, pp. 43, 133-34, 158; M'Cheyne, *OTS*, pp. 22-23; M'Cheyne, *TPH*, pp. 263, 270, 350; M'Cheyne, *TPP*, p. 140; M'Cheyne, *SOH*, p. 15.
19. Ibid., p. 172.

M'Cheyne's eschatology promoted a Christian piety consumed with living in light of eternity. A believer 'sees *eternity* as Christ does,' he asserted. 'Christ looked at everything in light of eternity.'[20] Therefore, 'believers should look on everything in light of eternity.'[21]

The promise of eternity with Christ gave M'Cheyne a purpose for pursuing holiness and a heavenly homesickness to his living. One Lord's Day, after preaching on Christ's second coming, he wrote, 'Felt its (Christ's imminent return) power myself more than ever before, how the sudden coming of the Saviour constrains to a holy walk separate from sin.'[22] How can a Christian tarry in sin when Christ could appear at any moment? Looking at life through the lens of eternity kept Christ ever before the eye, and so enabled the believer to keep a close communion with Him. One motive for holiness that he urged on his hearers focused on heavenly rewards. 'Christians will differ as one star from another in glory,' he reminded. 'Some will have an entrance, some an abundant entrance. Every lust indulged is lessening your eternal glory. Oh! will you give away something of heaven for that base lust?'[23]

Thus, as with all parts of his piety, M'Cheyne's eschatology-shaped spirituality centered on Christ. 'May we be among the number of those who "love his appearing," who are "looking for that blessed hope," and who are "waiting for his Son from heaven, even Jesus, which delivered us from the wrath to come." Surely they have but cold love to Jesus that do not burn with desire to see the fair brow that was crowned with thorns,' he wrote in a popular magazine.[24] A heart that loves Christ longs to be with Christ. M'Cheyne's piety embodied the apostle Paul's cry: 'For to me to live is Christ, and to die is gain.'

## Conclusion

M'Cheyne normally sealed his letters with the motto, 'The Night Cometh.' Eschatology, truth about the last things, was ever on his mind. Perhaps what is most compelling about M'Cheyne's living-in-light-of-

---

20. Ibid., p. 416 (emphasis original).
21. M'Cheyne, *TPH*, p. 199.
22. Bonar, *MAR*, p. 82.
23. M'Cheyne, *NTS*, p. 279.
24. Ibid., *HTD*, p. 1.

the-end ministry is that which was most ordinary in his pastorate: Christ was at the center.

His friendship with Andrew Bonar brought him into close contact with Edward Irving's millenarian agenda. These two influences were known not only for their deep thinking on prophecy, but also for the tendency to divide otherwise like-minded Christians. It is thus striking that M'Cheyne had so much affinity for their views but was able to minister them without discord. He knew eschatology should not create division or affliction. Looking to Jesus' near return should fuel an ever-deepening affection for the Savior. He believed that 'they are happiest who are living only for eternity, who have no object in this world to divert their hearts from Christ.'[25]

Such happiness was palpable in M'Cheyne's life. He spoke as one on the brink of eternity. The weight of Christ's eternal glory brought gravity and urgency to his life that many found attractive, even when it meant he constantly confronted his people with eternal things.

Eschatology and eternity were truths to increase obedience to Christ and express love for Him. A life lived in love for Jesus was M'Cheyne's primary concern. He wielded every part of Scripture to that end – even his view of the last things.

---

25. Bonar, *MAR*, p. 463.

CHAPTER 10

# Lessons Learned Along the Way

ALEXANDER Moody-Stuart was taken with Robert Murray M'Cheyne from their first meeting. 'It was to me a golden day when I first became acquainted with a young man so full of Christ,' Moody-Stuart recalled.[1] I feel the same.

Although I had heard his name mentioned in sermons and seen his story referenced in passing, I did not pay any real attention to M'Cheyne until 29 December 2007. I remember the day well. My future in-laws had invited me and my now wife, Emily, to the Alamo Bowl to watch their beloved Texas A&M Aggies battle on the gridiron. The drive from Weatherford to San Antonio is about four and a half hours long. I brought a book in case the car became quiet.

At the time, I was a young youth pastor eager to improve as a preacher. A friend had encouraged me, 'You have to read The Doctor's book on preaching.' On that December day so long ago, as the afternoon sun and engine's calming rumble lulled my future wife to sleep, I cracked open Martyn Lloyd-Jones' *Preaching and Preachers*. I eventually came to his lecture on 'The Act of Preaching.' He kept mentioning M'Cheyne. The first instance arrested my attention. 'You remember what was said of the saintly Robert Murray McCheyne of Scotland in the last century,' Lloyd-Jones began. 'It is said that when he appeared in the pulpit, even

---

1. Marjory Bonar, *Reminiscences*, p. x.

159

before he had uttered a single word, people would begin to weep silently. Why? Because of this very element of seriousness. The very sight of the man gave the impression that he had come from the presence of God and that he was to deliver a message from God to them.'[2]

I did not remember this story; I had never heard it. I knew nothing about this kind of preaching. I knew enough to think, 'This is what we need in the pulpit.' Those sentences put M'Cheyne's name on my mind's map. I only needed to read a few more chapters to realize he was a man I needed to analyze in detail.

I was not just a young pastor who desired to preach better; I was also desperate to know my Bible better. Yet my devotional habits were altogether dissatisfying. There was no rhythm in my practice. It was all fits and starts. Too many of the Bible's green pastures had gone untrod in my life. Thus, when Lloyd-Jones wrote about 'The Preparation of the Preacher' and focused on 'the next essential in the preacher's life – the reading of the Bible,' I was ready for his counsel. Lo and behold, for Lloyd-Jones, the exemplar of regular devotion in God's Word was M'Cheyne. The Doctor recalled:

> I remember how after I had worked out a scheme for myself and the members of my church in my early years in the ministry, I then came across the scheme that Robert Murray M'Cheyne worked out for the members of his church in Dundee. It is in his biography by Andrew Bonar. By following that scheme of Robert Murray M'Cheyne you read four chapters of the Bible every day, and by so doing you read the Old Testament once, but the Psalms and the New Testament twice, each year. Unlike many modern schemes he did not just pick out little sections, or a few verses or small paragraphs here and there, and thus take many years to go through the whole Bible, and in some cases omit certain passages altogether. The whole object of his scheme is to get people to go right through the Scriptures every year omitting nothing. That should be the very minimum of the preacher's Bible reading.[3]

I thought, 'If that is the bare minimum in the preacher's Bible reading, maybe that is one reason why my preaching is so minimal in its power.'

---

2. Lloyd-Jones, p. 86.
3. Ibid., p. 172.

I had never read the Bible from cover to cover in a year. I am not even sure if I had read every page of the Bible.

Three days later, 1 January 2008, my friendship with M'Cheyne began. I printed off a copy of his Bible reading plan and have used it ever since. I bought Andrew Bonar's *Memoir and Remains of Robert Murray M'Cheyne*. When it arrived, I devoured it in a few sittings. I knew I had found a soulmate in ministry. In 2015, I began my PhD studies. 'Do you know what you want to study?' Dr Michael Haykin asked in the initial interview. I replied, 'Robert Murray M'Cheyne.' 'What in particular about M'Cheyne do you want to study?' Dr Haykin responded. I do not remember my exact answer because I did not have an exact idea. I only recall stumbling over my words and providing immense proof of my scholarly inadequacies. Gratefully, the faculty welcomed me and let me examine M'Cheyne in minute detail.

I consider M'Cheyne's ministry magnetic. For the last twelve years, he has been a daily companion and helper. He is never boring or dry; he is always edifying and challenging. In fact, the Lord has – on no small number of occasions – used him to renew my strength in the gospel ministry. Let me tell you how by mentioning several lessons I have learned in my M'Cheyne studies.

## (1) The Centrality of Love for Christ

M'Cheyne was a living embodiment of the apostle's cry, 'For the love of Christ controls us' (2 Cor. 5:14). No other pulsebeat in ministry can sustain the pastor. No other passion will suffice. Only the love of Christ, worked in the soul by God's Spirit, can animate a ministry that speaks life into dead bones.

No small number of false motives exist in ministry – money, security, and respectability are common. One of the most troubling in our time is the desire to grow one's personal platform. The temptation is not new. Obtaining a platform is, however, far easier today than in previous generations. The internet's ubiquity allows pastors to attract an international audience in a way that was previously impossible. Social media's visibility allows preachers to reach untold number of souls. It is one thing to receive a platform; it is another thing entirely to seek a platform. Platform-building is a most noxious display of self-love. It longs to glorify self instead of the Savior. It also burns pastors easily as such self-love never brings contentment. When your greatest passion is more listens, more likes, and more numbers, your motivating power is one that can never satisfy. It is a harsh taskmaster that only drives the soul into the ministerial ground.

M'Cheyne knew this temptation well. He often commented in his diary about his attraction to people's praise. Recall his entry after ministry on a Lord's Day: 'Some tears; yet I fear some like the messenger, not the message; and I fear I am so vain as to love that love. Lord, let it not be so. Perish *my* honour, but let *Thine* be exalted forever.'[4]

Much better is love for Christ. What the world needs is not men of personality or ability, but men reveling in Jesus Christ. We need preachers ravished with Christ's beauty and majesty. The Christ-loving minister is the man who knows true joy and rest. He drinks daily from the inexhaustible fountain of grace and truth. His deepest cries are for communion with Christ: 'Let him kiss me with the kisses of his mouth! For your love is better than wine; your anointing oils are fragrant; your name is oil poured out ... Draw me after you; let us run' (Song 1:2-4).

'The righteousness of Christ is a million times more lovely than that of the highest angel,' M'Cheyne announced.[5] Faithful pastors say, 'Yes and amen.' He thus realized the apostolic goal not only of 2 Corinthians 5:14 but also Philippians 3:3-11. His early life of prosperity and privilege were nothing compared to Christ. He laid it all aside because of the surpassing worth of loving Jesus Christ – knowing Him, gaining Him, and being found in Him.

## (2) The Priority of Prayer

Prayer is the power that moves Him who holds the universe. When preaching brought little fruit, M'Cheyne pointed his friends to the unfailing power of prayer. 'When preaching fails,' he told the Reverend Miller, 'try prayer.'[6] Prayer is the first half of our ministry and gives the second half all its strength.

---

4. Bonar, *MAR*, p. 44.
5. Ibid., p. 387.
6. Ibid., p. 323.

Maybe one reason why we search in vain for mighty preachers is because there are so few in the gospel ministry who are mighty in prayer. William Williams of Wern, a giant of the Welsh pulpit in M'Cheyne's time, commented:

> The old ministers were not much better preachers than we are, and in many respects they were inferior, but there was an unction about their ministry, and success attended upon it now but seldom witnessed. And what was the cause of the difference? They *prayed* more than we do. If we would prevail and have power with men, we must first prevail and have power with God. It was on his knees that Jacob became a prince, and if we would become princes we must be oftener and more importunate upon our knees.[7]

Where are the pastors today who are known first as mighty in prayer?

Our Savior commanded us to pray in secret (Matt. 6:5-6). It is thus entirely possible that many ministers today are familiar with secret prayer, but we don't know it because they obediently keep their practice to themselves. If my personal experience and pastoral observance are representative, we should conclude most ministers' practice of prayer is not what it should be.

M'Cheyne knew a prayerless ministry leads to a paralyzed pulpit. He was genuinely dumbfounded when someone asked him if his parish duties limited his time in prayer. 'What would my people do if I were not to pray?' he replied.[8]

When ministers devote themselves to prayer, it will not take long for such dependence to overflow in public. Prayer will saturate the Lord's Day gathering. Corporate prayer meetings will again flourish. Spontaneous prayer will erupt in family worship, small group gatherings, and one-to-one settings. The lifeblood of the church will again course through the congregation's veins. And it must start with the preacher.

M'Cheyne's practice also warns pastors away from preaching in their prayers. Extant commentary on his public prayer speaks to his striking familiarity with the throne of grace. He was ever mindful not to turn prayer into preaching. Andrew Bonar knew how often the preacher's public prayer turned into sermonizing. He recorded in his diary: 'I saw

---

7. Quoted in Murphy, *Pastoral Theology*, p. 32 (emphasis original).
8. Bonar, *MAR*, p. 51. See also, *MAR*, p. 547.

... that in prayer the speaker ought to try to move the heart of God and not the feelings of man, and that I should be much more fervent in private prayer.'[9] Real eloquence in public prayer always begins with diligence in the prayer closet. Perhaps the public prayer in our churches is weak precisely because we have neglected secret prayer.

Prayer remains the truest test of one's spirituality. It is the energy behind growing piety.

## (3) The Need for Personal Holiness

God blesses likeness to Jesus more than great talents. What every congregation needs from their leaders, more than anything else, is vital godliness.

We cannot let fear of potential legalism squelch the biblical demand: pastors must be holy. Our usefulness in the ministry depends on our purity. As Paul exhorted Timothy, 'If anyone cleanses himself from what is dishonorable, he will be a vessel for honorable use, set apart as holy, useful to the master of the house, ready for every good work' (2 Tim. 2:21). God loves to use holy ministers. The Lord delights to employ those who are humble toward Him and hungry for truth. The word translated as 'vessel' is one that was used for a household utensil. Just as a knife is not useful to eat Lucky Charms or a plate is not useful to hold your morning coffee, so does a lack of holiness mean a preacher is not useful to the Lord or ready for every good work.

The point M'Cheyne would have us understand is that without personal holiness, we have no reason to expect God's blessing in our ministry. Could God bless our churches in spite of our small devotion to Christ? Absolutely. And praise God for doing it often! Nevertheless, we cannot expect fruit will grow unless holiness flowers in our soul.

You'll remember how Paul speaks to Timothy in 2 Timothy 3:16-17, reminding the Ephesians' pastor that 'all Scripture is breathed out by God and profitable for teaching, for reproof, for correction, and for training in righteousness, that the man of God may be complete, equipped for every good work.' We rightly emphasize this text in our doctrine of Scripture. We also are correct to use it as a proof text for biblical preaching and

---

9. Bonar, *Diary and Letters*, p. 39.

teaching. We should not, however, gloss over the title Paul uses for the pastor: the man of God. Such a title was used of Moses, Joshua, and other mighty men in the Old Testament. Here it is used of an ordinary pastor. Maybe, then, pastors are not so ordinary after all. At least they shouldn't be! They must be men eminent in holiness, reflecting Christ's image with unusual luster and brilliance. They must be men of God. Or, taken in a different way, they must be men of Christ. It is the man of Christ who will best proclaim the message of Christ. Only when the preacher shakes and quakes with love for Jesus will he reach his full power in preaching. Christlikeness is thus the personality of true preachers.

M'Cheyne's instruction, especially to pastors, is that while the world looks for better methods to grow the church, God looks for better men. They are His chosen tools to shape His church after Christ.

## (4) The Power of Sincerity

David Robertson, in his biography of M'Cheyne, wonders, 'Perhaps a key to McCheyne's success is due to his sincerity and transparency.'[10] I am more certain: sincerity was a primary factor in his labor.

Sincerity in ministry is the apostolic ideal. 'For our boast is this, the testimony of our conscience,' Paul admits to the Corinthians, 'that we behaved in the world with simplicity and godly sincerity, not by earthly wisdom but by the grace of God' (2 Cor. 1:12). He further explains: 'We are not, like so many, peddlers of God's word, but as men of sincerity, as commissioned by God, in the sight of God we speak in Christ' (2 Cor. 2:17).

Let us rightly treasure sincerity in the ministry. It gives luster and beauty to every prayer, sermon, and conversation. A genuine spirit overcomes doubters and opponents. Honesty and humility is the twin-engine driving sincerity. When such virtues thrive in the pastor's heart, he is well on his way to fruitfulness. Whenever they wither, however, hypocrisy and formality stain the minister's actions. Few sins upset our Savior more than a false mask of spirituality (e.g., Matt. 23). Unfeigned humility and Spirit-dependent sincerity must be the pastor's constant longing.

---

10. David Robertson, *Awakening*, p. 23.

We dare not fall into Satan's lie in thinking we can fool God's people. Sermons can be formally tight, but the church can see when the heart is not right. Prayers may be carefully scripted, but a congregation can tell when the pastor knows nothing of communion before the throne. Today's generation, which esteems authenticity, sees through a false veneer of piety. An open heart wins hearts. Preaching that reaches the heart must come from the heart. 'The plainest truths,' Archibald Alexander lectured, 'will have an effect upon most men when the speaker gives manifest indication of being sincere in all that he says.'[11]

M'Cheyne learned the beauty of sincerity from his eldest brother. David M'Cheyne's religion had appeal to his siblings precisely because it was genuine. His life's pattern confirmed every plea, prayer, and counsel as sincere. Robert's poem, 'On Painting the Miniature Likeness of One Departed,' tried to capture the power of David's witness. One section points to the effect of David's genuineness of spirit:

> And oh! recall the look of faith sincere,
> With which that eye would scrutinize the page
> That tells us of offended God appeased
> By awful sacrifice upon the cross
> Of Calvary – that bids us leave a world
> Immersed in darkness and death, and seek
> A better country. Ah! how oft that eye
> Would turn on me, with pity's tenderest look,
> And, only half-upbraiding, bid me flee
> From the vain idols of my boyish heart![12]

A faithful pulpit ministry must exude many spiritual fruits: patience, joy, reverence, and boldness. Before all these must come a sincere love, which is the aim of our charge (1 Tim. 1:5). Without such honesty our preaching will be as melodious as the cacophony of children banging spoons on pots. This is why M'Cheyne exhorted William Chalmers Burns:

> I charge you, be clothed with humility, or you will yet be a wandering star, for which is reserved the blackness of darkness forever. Let Christ increase; let man decrease. This is my constant prayer for myself and you. If you lead

---

11. Quoted in Garretson, p. 187.
12. Bonar, *MAR*, pp. 6-7.

sinners to yourself, and not to Christ, Immanuel will cast the star out of His right hand into utter darkness. Remember what I said of preaching out of the Scriptures: honour the word both in matter and manner.[13]

Sincerity is the first characteristic of a faithful and fruitful manner in preaching. M'Cheyne knew this and ministered accordingly. No wonder his efforts possessed such power.

## (5) The Value of Friendship

If the spiritual gift of friendship exists, M'Cheyne had it. 'A book might be dedicated to the subject of McCheyne's friendships,' concludes one biographer.[14] Robert was a central figure in what became known as 'The M'Cheyne Group.' The informal network included mighty men such as Alexander Moody-Stuart, John Milne, James Hamilton, William Chalmers Burns, Alexander Somerville, and the Bonar brothers. The M'Cheyne School shared a ministerial philosophy filled with Christ. They toiled for Christ through a collective focus on piety, prayer, preaching, revival, and missionary activity. Although small, the group exercised an outsized influence on the evangelical wing of the Church of Scotland, and later, in the Free Church of Scotland.

M'Cheyne's friendships were vital to his ministry. Constant encouragement and counsel from friends sustained him through seasons of affliction. He responded in turn. His extant letters exude a devotion to brothers in Christ rarely seen in today's context. M'Cheyne poured out his soul to his friends. He was always faithful to pray for his friends' ministries and needs. He was a friend who loved at all times and was born for adversity (Prov. 17:17).

Friendship in the gospel has a way of undercutting competition in ministry. When you know a fellow minister intimately, it is much harder to fall into the snare of jealousy. Especially when you give yourself to pray for a friend's preaching, you will notice affection rise in your soul.

The world knows we belong to Jesus by our love for each other (John 13:35). Friendship in the Lord thus has an apologetic value. It also is crucial in our congregations as well. How many churches today

---

13. Ibid., p. 130.
14. Smellie, p. 53.

would grow in the bonds of peace if they saw and heard their pastor's love for ministers in other churches, other denominations? What unity would thrive as pastors care for and serve each other in visible ways?

## (6) The Longing for Revival

The quality of insatiability marked M'Cheyne's ministry. His constant heart-cry was, 'More!' More of Christ! More of the Spirit! More souls won to the Savior! Such desires converged in his passion for revival. 'Oh, let us pray that what is past may be but the beginning of days to our thirsty land! Let us stretch out our souls for more. ... Would it not be to Immanuel's honour to come and reveal Himself in such a way that no man could take any of the praise? Oh to be humble and believing and expecting!' he cried.[15] From the earliest days of his ministry, revival was on his mind. He prayed for it, read stories of it, and exhorted his people to watch for it.

I may be wrong, but a hunger for the Spirit's outpouring does not resound from many ministers today. Perhaps our small appetite for revival is due to the excesses of revivalism. We have seen and have heard stories of enthusiasm's excess. Yet, abuse does not remove use. David declares, 'Your people will offer themselves freely on the day of your power' (Ps. 110:3). The Spirit's dawning is a day of power. Such appearances and awakenings punctuate the gospel's advance. Do we not still hope for the gospel to arrive 'in power and in the Holy Spirit and with full conviction' (1 Thess. 1:5)?

M'Cheyne speculated to Andrew Bonar that one reason they had not seen revival was because they were not ready for it. Is the same true of today's ordinary pastor? Maybe we are not ready to counsel people through their heavy consciences. Maybe we have become dull to the possibility of extraordinary outpourings of God's Spirit. Perhaps we do not have because we do not ask.

Passion for revival reveals important realities. Understood correctly, revival is a sovereign work of God's Spirit. No new measures or pragmatic strategies guarantee success. It is the Spirit's work alone. He blows wherever and whenever He wills. The pastor who prays earnestly

---

15. Bonar, *The Life of John Milne*, p. 35.

for revival is a pastor who pants for a shower of the sovereign Spirit. That minister also shows himself dependent on the Spirit. Few things reveal one's longing for and leaning on the Spirit like revival prayer. We pray for it because we want to know the measure of His power. We yearn for it because we want an experience of His love.

Calvinism is no wet blanket to God's reviving work. The doctrines of grace are the best theological interpreters of the Spirit's awakening. Preaching the Father's sovereign grace in Jesus Christ, in humble reliance on the Spirit, is the ordinary means to bring about an extraordinary outpouring. M'Cheyne's ministry proved the point. Thus, J. W. Alexander could exclaim of him: 'What zeal and faith! What a proof that Old Calvinism is not insusceptible of being used as an arousing instrument!'[16]

## (7) The Gravity of Eternity

One week after graduating from the Divinity Hall, M'Cheyne recorded in his journal, 'Life is vanishing fast. Make haste for eternity.'[17] His lifelong battles with illness, and a frail immune system, convinced him that a long life was not his lot. His flame would burn hot and fast for Jesus Christ.

Eternity weighed heavily on his mind. He knew he would give an account to Christ for the way he preached and pastored. His self-examination led to much lament. He did not consider his preaching urgent enough; he thought he should be more zealous in calling souls to Christ. One's life can end in an instant. The Day of Judgment was on the way. These realities affected his ministry. They infused his labors with a gravity and urgency that only eternity can incite.

One of the most common criticisms made today of M'Cheyne is that he did not rest enough. He supposedly worked too hard. 'He worked himself to death,' the criticism goes. Such censure reveals how comfortable and complacent we have become. The critique also does not reckon with the many weeks – even months – that he was out of the pulpit. Much of this rest was forced inactivity due to illness. His days on

16. Hall, 2:11.
17. Bonar, *MAR*, p. 26.

the sickbed only further solidified the conviction that sealed his letters: 'The night cometh.' Did he expend himself for Christ? Undoubtedly. But should not every minister agonize for Jesus Christ? The ministry may not kill us, but it should certainly exhaust us. The apostle Paul believed striving, toil, and agony are hallmarks of Christian ministry. He commended Epaphras to the Colossians as 'a faithful minister' who was 'always struggling on your behalf in his prayers, that you may stand mature and fully assured in all the will of God. For I bear him witness that he has worked hard for you' (Col. 4:12-13). The words Paul uses underscores the exertion he values in gospel ministry. 'Struggling' is more literally 'agonize.' The language of 'work hard' is rare in the Pauline writings; it is the language of pain. One commentator explains: 'Paul has ... chosen a word that highlights the difficulty and degree of exertion involved in the "work" that Epaphras is doing for the Colossians.'[18]

Let us discover how eternity's magnitude fuels faithful ministers, increasing exertion and earnestness. Richard Baxter once penned a poem titled, 'Love Breathing Thanks and Praise.' The verses contain famous sentiments about ministering in light of eternity.

> This called me out to work while it was day;
> And warn poor souls to turn without delay:
> Resolving speedily thy Word to preach,
> With Ambrose I at once did learn and teach.
> Still thinking I had little time to live,
> My fervent heart to win men's souls did strive.
> *I preached as never sure to preach again,*
> *And as a dying man to dying men!*
> O how should preachers men's repenting crave
> Who see how near the Church is to the grave?
> And see that while we preach and hear, we die,
> Rapt by swift time to vast eternity![19]

Robert Murray M'Cheyne was a dying man who ministered to dying men. May we learn from his example and so grow in our faithfulness.

---

18. Moo, p. 346.
19. Baxter, p. 35.

# Bibliography

Richard Baxter (1681), *The Poetical Fragments of Richard Baxter*, William Pickering.

David P. Beaty (2014), *An All-Surpassing Fellowship: Learning from Robert Murray M'Cheyne's Communion with God*, Reformation Heritage Books.

William Garden Blaikie (rpt. 2001), *The Preachers of Scotland: From the Sixth to the Nineteenth Century*, Banner of Truth.

Andrew A. Bonar (1960), *Andrew Bonar: Diary and Life*, Banner of Truth.

Andrew A. Bonar (1844), *Memoir and Remains of the Rev. Robert Murray M'Cheyne*, Paul T. Jones.

Andrew A. Bonar (1844, rpt. 2012), *Robert Murray M'Cheyne*, Banner of Truth.

Horatius Bonar (1869, rpt. 2010), *Life of John Milne*, Banner of Truth.

Marjory Bonar, ed. (1894), *Andrew A. Bonar, D.D., Diary and Letters*, Hodder and Stoughton.

Marjory Bonar, ed. (1895), *Reminiscences of Andrew A. Bonar, D.D.*, Hodder and Stoughton.

David Brown (1872), *Life of the Late John Duncan, LL.D.: Professor of Hebrew and Oriental Languages, New College, Edinburgh*, Edmonston and Douglas.

Ralph Brown (2007), 'Victorian Anglican Evangelicalism: The Radical Legacy of Edward Irving,' *The Journal of Ecclesiastical History* 58, no. 4 (October 2007).

Stewart J. Brown (1982), *Thomas Chalmers and the Godly Commonwealth in Scotland*, Oxford University Press.

Robert Buchanan (1849), *The Ten Years' Conflict: Being the History of the Disruption of the Church of Scotland*, Blackie and Son.

Nigel M. de S. Cameron et al (1993), *Dictionary of Scottish Church History and Theology*, InterVarsity.

D. A. Carson (1998), *For the Love of God*, Vol. 1, IVP, 11-25.

Thomas Chalmers (1852), *Daily Scripture Readings*, Vol. 3, Thomas Constable and Co.

A. Cheyne (1999), *Studies in Scottish Church History*, T&T Clark.

James Dodds (1887), *Personal Reminiscences and Biographical Sketches*, Macniven & Wallace.

Andrew L. Drummond and James Bulloch (1975), *The Church in Victorian Scotland, 1843–1874*, Saint Andrews Press.

Alexander Dunlop (1846), *Sermons by the Late Reverend David Welsh D.D. with a Memoir*, W. P. Kennedy.

William Gerald Enright (1968), 'Preaching and Theology in Scotland in the Nineteenth Century: A Study of the Context and the Content of the Evangelical Sermon' (Ph.D. thesis, University of Edinburgh).

Michael Fry (1991), *Patronage and Principle: A Political History of Modern Scotland*, Aberdeen University Press.

James Garretson (2015), *Thoughts on Preaching and Pastoral Ministry*, Reformation Heritage Books

Crawford Gribben (2004), 'Andrew Bonar and the Scottish Presbyterian Millennium,' in *Prisoners of Hope? Aspects of Evangelical Millennialism in Britain and Ireland, 1800–1880*, ed. Crawford Gribben and Timothy C. F. Stunt, Paternoster.

John Hall (1860), *Forty Years' Familiar Letters of James W. Alexander* (New York: Charles Scribner, 1860; repr., Laurel, Miss: Audubon Press, 2008).

James Hamilton (1847), *The Church in the House: And Other Tracts*, James Nisbet.

James Hastings, ed. (1897), *The Expository Times: Vol. 8*, T. & T. Clark.

John Angell James (1847, rpt. 1993), *An Earnest Ministry*, Banner of Truth.

Marcus Loane (2006), *They Were Pilgrims,* Banner of Truth.

D. Martyn Lloyd-Jones (1971), *Preaching and Preachers*, Hodder & Stoughton.

John Macleod (1943, rpt. 1974), *Scottish Theology in Relation to Church History*, Banner of Truth.

Robert Murray M'Cheyne (1848, rpt. 1975), *A Basket of Fragments*, Christian Focus.

Robert Murray M'Cheyne, ed. Adam M'Cheyne (1849), *Familiar Letters by the Rev. Robert Murray M'Cheyne: Containing an Account of His Travels as One of the Deputation Sent Out by the Church of Scotland on a Mission of Inquiry to the Jews in 1839*, Robert Carter.

Robert Murray M'Cheyne (1846, rpt. 1993), *From the Preacher's Heart*, Christian Focus.

Robert Murray M'Cheyne (2004), *New Testament Sermons*, Banner of Truth.

Robert Murray M'Cheyne (2004), *Old Testament Sermons*, Banner of Truth.

Robert Murray M'Cheyne (1999), *The Passionate Preacher: Sermons of Robert Murray McCheyne*, Christian Focus Publications.

Robert Murray M'Cheyne (1858, rpt. 1987), *The Believer's Joy*, Free Presbyterian Publications.

Donald K. McKim, David F. Wright eds. (1992), *Encyclopedia of the Reformed Faith*, Westminster/John Knox Press.

Douglas J. Moo (2008), *The Letters to the Colossians and to Philemon*, Grand Rapids: Eerdmans.

Alexander Moody-Stuart (1872), *Recollections of the Late John Duncan, LL.D.: Professor of Hebrew and Oriental Languages, New College, Edinburgh*, Edmonston and Douglas.

Iain H. Murray (2006), *A Scottish Christian Heritage*, Banner of Truth.

Hughes Oliphant Old (2007), *The Reading and Preaching of the Scriptures in the Worship of the Christian Church*, Baker.

Derek Prime (2007), *Robert Murray McCheyne: In the Footsteps of a Godly Scottish Pastor*. Leominster, UK: Day One.

C. J. A. Robertson (1978), 'Early Scottish Railways and the Observance of the Sabbath,' *The Scottish Historical Review* 57, no. 164.

David Robertson (2004), *Awakening: The Life and Ministry of Robert Murray McCheyne*, Christian Focus.

Alexander Smellie (rpt. 2005), *R. M. M'Cheyne*, Christian Focus Publications.

George Smith (1890), *A Modern Apostle: Alexander N. Somerville, 1813–1889*, Murray.

C. H. Spurgeon (1890), *Lectures to My Students: A Selection from Addresses Delivered to the Students of the Pastors' College, Metropolitan Tabernacle, London*, Robert Carter & Brothers.

Jordan Stone (2019), *A Communion of Love: The Christ-Centered Spirituality of Robert Murray M'Cheyne*, Wipf & Stock.

L. J. Van Valen (2002), *Constrained By His Love*, A New Biography of Robert Murray McCheyne. Christian Focus Publications.

David Victor Yeaworth (1975), 'Robert Murray M'Cheyne (1813–1843): A Study of an Early Nineteenth-Century Scottish Evangelical' (Ph.D. diss, University of Edinburgh).

# Index

Also available from Christian Focus Publications...

# The
# Believer's
# Joy

## Robert Murray
## McCheyne

# The Believer's Joy

## R. M. McCheyne

Robert Murray McCheyne's fervent love of the gospel shone clearly through everything he wrote and said, often leading him to tears while he preached. This short book brings together seven such sermons, in which McCheyne expounds the glories of life in Christ. Shorter and more easily digestible than some of his written works, but lacking none of the biblical depth, these sermons make for powerful devotional material.

*In the absence of a recording device from the 1830s when McCheyne was minister, these pages provide the next best thing – the text of several sermons McCheyne prepared for the people he loved so dearly. They bear all the hallmarks of all his preaching – simplicity, clarity, directness, earnestness, Christ–centredness, and in addition a certain pathos and poetic beauty. No matter what age or stage of the Christian life you may have reached, you will find yourself spiritually nourished and drawn to Christ by what you read here.*

Sinclair B. Ferguson
Chancellor's Professor of Systematic Theology, Reformed
Theological Seminary, Jackson, Mississippi

ISBN 978-1-5271-0148-7

# A
# Basket
## of
# Fragments
## Notes for Revival

### Robert Murray
# McCheyne

# A Basket of Fragments

## Notes for Revival

## R. M. McCheyne

Robert Murray McCheyne lived only until his thirtieth year, and yet his preaching continues to impact generations of believers. In the years following his death, his congregation compiled a collection of his sermons from their own personal notes, so eager were they to preserve his writings.

The result is a collection of bite-size sermons characterised by Christ-centred exposition, that testifies to McCheyne's trust in the Word of God. *A Basket of Fragments* overflows with wisdom stemming from a love of Scripture and a passionate desire to see people saved. Each portion of clear yet poetic teaching, when savoured, will produce lasting spiritual nourishment.

*Since my childhood, Robert Murray McCheyne has been a family hero, as he has been throughout Scotland and in many parts of the world.* A Basket of Fragments *is one of the first books published by Christian Focus, over forty years ago. It is a treasure.*

*Read and you will see why. Here is heart-warming Gospel clarity with the passion of a loving heart. Saints comforted, sinners warned, Christ glorified and the cross of Christ central. Experience the record of holy unction, fervour, wisdom and love. As you read this, you will understand why my grandfather (whom I never met) cherished three books: The Bible,* Pilgrim's Progress *and* A Basket of Fragments.

*I believe you will cherish this book also.*

William H. M. Mackenzie
Managing Director, Christian Focus Publications

ISBN 978-1-5271-0269-9

"...a fine and fresh account of a great
and godly minister of the gospel."
Eric Alexander

AWAKENING
THE LIFE & MINISTRY OF
ROBERT MURRAY MᶜCHEYNE

David Robertson

# Awakening

## The Life and Ministry of Robert Murray McCheyne

### David Robertson

Was McCheyne for real? Was he just famous because he died so young? Does he have anything to teach us today? In this book, David Robertson, a former minister of McCheyne's church, St Peter's in Dundee, Scotland, seeks to answer these and other questions. Through the use of published sermons, private papers and historical material, this contemporary devotional biography traces McCheyne's life and influence from his upbringing, conversion and training for the ministry to the revival that occurred in St. Peter's in 1839 and his early death. The contemporary relevance of McCheyne for today's church is demonstrated and the glory of God is seen in this wonderful story of what He can do with one 'consecrated sinner'.

*...a fine and fresh account of a great and godly minister of the gospel. David Robertson gives us new insight into McCheyne's personal life, and his preparation for preaching, his deep social concern and his absolute devotion to the glory of God as the ultimate motive of everything he did.*

Eric Alexander
Conference speaker and formerly minister, St George's Tron, Glasgow

ISBN 978-1-8455-0542-4

# RUNNING THE RACE

## ERIC LIDDELL
### OLYMPIC CHAMPION & MISSIONARY

# Running the Race

## Eric Liddell – Olympic Champion and Missionary

## John W. Keddie

The name Eric Liddell is a familiar one to many, having gained much fame through the film *Chariots of Fire*. A Christian athlete and missionary, his passion for his Saviour could be seen throughout his life. From university days to internment at Weihsien POW Camp, John Keddie's biography brings together a specialist understanding of both Liddell's faith and sporting achievements to provide an engaging account of this normal man's extraordinary life.

*Former athlete and churchman John Keddie brings both sporting expertise and spiritual insight to this lucid and meticulous biography of the great Eric Liddell.*

Sally Magnusson
Broadcaster (Reporting Scotland, Songs of Praise) & Author of several books, including *The Flying Scotsman: The Eric Liddell Story*

*Running the Race is the definitive biography of Eric Liddell and one can say with confidence that Liddell himself would have approved. Not only is John Keddie the foremost authority on Scottish athletics, but he is also a Presbyterian Minister uniquely placed to set Liddell's sporting achievements in the context of the bigger priority of his Christian faith and witness. This superbly researched book inspires on many levels.*

Peter Lovesey
Crime writer & Athletics historian; National Union of Track Statisticians member

ISBN 978-1-5271-0531-7

A RADICAL,
COMPREHENSIVE

CALL
*to*
HOLINESS

*Joel R. Beeke &*
*Michael P. V. Barrett*

# A Radical, Comprehensive Call to Holiness

## Joel R. Beeke and Michael P. V. Barrett

The mandate for holiness is based in the very character and person of God: we are to be holy because God is holy. His grace never leaves a man where it finds him. Grace always transforms the sinner into a saint—a holy man. God's will is for His people to be holy, and the explanations of why and how we become holy are throughout the Bible.

*Explaining the tension between positional and progressive holiness, Joel Beeke and Michael Barrett expound the doctrine of sanctification and show that it is the application of the gospel to our daily lives. If you've ever considered why, if we are saved by grace alone, holiness matters, this book is for you.*

*In recent days, we have witnessed a renewed interest in Reformed theology, and in this we rejoice. But there is one area that has been sadly overlooked and needs to be addressed, namely, the doctrine of sanctification. This book,* A Radical, Comprehensive Call to Holiness, *provides the necessary antidote to this omission. Well-designed and thoroughly studied, this volume by Drs. Joel Beeke and Michael Barrett is certain to be a valuable and trusted aid in your Christian walk.*

Steven J. Lawson
President, OnePassion Ministries and Professor of Preaching,
The Master's Seminary, Sun Valley, California

ISBN 978-1-5271-0611-6

# Christian Focus Publications

Our mission statement –

STAYING FAITHFUL

In dependence upon God we seek to impact the world through literature faithful to His infallible Word, the Bible. Our aim is to ensure that the Lord Jesus Christ is presented as the only hope to obtain forgiveness of sin, live a useful life and look forward to heaven with Him.

Our books are published in four imprints:

### CHRISTIAN
## FOCUS

Popular works including biographies, commentaries, basic doctrine and Christian living.

### CHRISTIAN
## HERITAGE

Books representing some of the best material from the rich heritage of the church.

## MENTOR

Books written at a level suitable for Bible College and seminary students, pastors, and other serious readers. The imprint includes commentaries, doctrinal studies, examination of current issues and church history.

## CF4•K

Children's books for quality Bible teaching and for all age groups: Sunday school curriculum, puzzle and activity books; personal and family devotional titles, biographies and inspirational stories – because you are never too young to know Jesus!

Christian Focus Publications Ltd,
Geanies House, Fearn, Ross-shire,
IV20 1TW, Scotland, United Kingdom.
www.christianfocus.com